I Know What I Want To Say
I Just Don't Know How To Say It

how to write essays, reports, blogs, presentations, books, proposals, memos, and other nonfiction

MARK HANEN

howtosayit.ca

©2014 Mark Hanen

This book is also available in electronic format. ISBN 978-0-9879307-1-2

Edited by Charlie Burton and Terri Hanen

Page design and typesetting by Kim Hanen
khanen@shaw.ca

Library and Archives Canada Cataloguing in Publication

Hanen, Mark, 1949-

Words : I know what I want to say, I just don't know how to say it :
how to write essays, reports, blogs, presentations, books, proposals,
memos, and other nonfiction / Mark Hanen.
ISBN 978-0-9879307-0-5

1. Authorship. 2. English language--Rhetoric. I. Title.

PE1408.H36 2013   808'.042   C2013-901715-1

JustOneWord Publishing

Canada

17   18   19   20

"No writing is a waste of time –
no creative work where the feelings,
the imagination,
the intelligence must work.

With every sentence you write,
you have learned something.
It has done you good."

— BRENDA UELAND

Introduction

Some are born writers, some achieve writing, and some have writing thrust upon them.

Is This Book For Me?

Words skillfully guides you, step by step, through your entire writing project. Written in a conversational style, it explains how to shape, focus, organize, and polish your non-fiction writing. It coaches you through the process of discovering what you want to say, how you want to say it, and how you convey your ideas with precision, clarity, and confidence.

Words is a clear, concise, well-organized book that quickly builds your skills and your confidence. It presents practical strategies, realistic techniques, and common sense guidelines for writing; it even sprinkles in a little humour. If you write books, proposals, essays, memos, reports, blogs, manuals, presentations, memoirs, articles, journals, or creative nonfiction, *Words* is the book for you.

Words is for writers who know what they want to say but do not know how to say it. It is for writers who do not know what they want to say. It is for born writers, aspiring writers, and for people who have writing thrust upon them.

If this is not the book for you, please note that it makes a thoughtful gift for all writers of nonfiction.

What Will I Learn?

Sometimes, you do not know what you want to say.

Thoughtful writing begins by discovering a single word.

Organized writing creates a single path and follows a single goal.

Establishing context is crucial because we all see the world in a slightly different way.

Nonfiction writers are like tour guides.

Balance, parallelism, and symmetry make writing accessible and enjoyable.

Using unnecessary words obscures your ideas.

The English language contains only four basic punctuation marks and three basic sentence types.

Common grammatical errors spoil your credibility.

A checklist is a writer's friend.

What Makes This Book Different?

This book explains the entire writing process from formulating your initial idea to reviewing your punctuation. It not only explains how to write, it explains how to think about writing.

The language is conversational; the approach is straightforward; the writing is concise; the ideas are fresh. Examples of effective writing come from diverse sources.

The book consolidates complex systems of grammar, punctuation, and usage into eleven simple rules.

The paragraphs are short.

Why Is The Book Called *Words*?

Imagine yourself living in 17th century England. The afternoon sun warms your skin as you hurry past stalls selling fish and fresh baked pies. You join thousands of boisterous theatregoers gathered outside The Globe theatre for a performance of Shakespeare's *Hamlet*.

Standing at the foot of the stage, crowded together with friends, pickpockets, and prostitutes, you see Hamlet on stage reading a book. Hamlet's cousin approaches and asks, "What are you reading, my lord?" Hamlet replies, "Words, words, words."

Everything we think, know, say, read, and write involves words.

Words make us human. Writing expresses our common humanity.

Knowing What You Want To Say

Before You Write

Before you start writing do three things: discover your keyword, determine your key idea, and understand your audience.

Your Keyword

Your keyword captures the heart, soul, and character of your subject. It is the one word that summarizes the essence of your thinking. Your subject might be the *true meaning of family*, but your keyword will be a single word such as loyalty, or trust, or friendship. Discovering your keyword concentrates and defines the core of your thinking.

Your Key Idea

Your key idea consists of your goal and your genre. Your goal is your purpose for writing expressed as a single action verb. Your genre is a recognizable framework such as comparison, classification, or definition. Together they form your key idea: This report *argues* that organic apples are superior to non-organic apples *by comparing* their taste, nutritional value, and texture. Determining your key idea organizes and unifies your writing.

Your Audience

Always express your ideas with honesty and integrity, but always respect your audience. Communication begins by acknowledging that we all see the world in a slightly different way. Understanding your audience is the beginning of communication.

Conclusion

Once you have identified your keyword, key idea, and audience, writing flows. Your keyword focuses your writing and determines, in part, your title. Your genre provides your organizational framework. Explaining and expressing the link between your goal and genre forms a large part of your introduction. And, acknowledging your audience informs your choice of vocabulary, supporting evidence, and overall approach. Writing in a coherent, logical, and organized manner depends on what you think about before you start writing.

ONE
Discover Your Keyword

To see a world in a grain of sand.

– William Blake

In the 1991 comedy, *City Slickers*, a trail hardened cowboy named Curly (Jack Palance) shares his philosophy of life with a city slicker named Mitch (Billy Crystal):

> Curly: "Do you know what the secret of life is? This."
> [Curly holds up one finger.]
>
> Mitch: "Your finger?"
>
> Curly: One thing. Just one thing. You stick to that and the rest don't mean shit.
>
> Mitch: But, what is the one thing?
>
> Curly: [He smiles.] That's what you have to find out.

Make the discussion about writing and words, and Curly provides us with the first step for writing nonfiction:

> Curly: Do you know what the secret of writing is? This.
> [Curly holds up one finger.]
>
> Mitch: Your finger?
>
> Curly: "One word. Just one word. You stick to that and the rest falls into place."
>
> Mitch: But, what is the one word?
>
> Curly: [He smiles.] That's what you have to find out."

That one word "you have to find out" is called your keyword. Knowing what you want to say, and knowing how to say it, starts with discovering this essential word.

Your keyword is not the same as your subject. Your keyword is the word that unlocks your subject and all of your other words and ideas.

It expresses the idea that lies at the heart of your writing. Your keyword propels your writing forward.

Having run out of excuses not to write, you sit at your desk or kitchen table when someone asks, "What are you writing about?" You hastily reply, "luxury yachts," or "Jennifer Aniston," or "marriage."

However, yachts, actresses, and marriage are subjects, not keywords. Thinking about a subject, your mind is full of words and ideas that dance and swirl in your brain like wind-blown autumn leaves. Making sense of all the data, for yourself and for your reader, begins with capturing the essence of your subject in a single keyword.

For example, if your subject is mutual funds, an overwhelming wealth of information presents itself. But once you discover that your keyword is *risk*, you have found your way forward. Similarly, marriage is a vast subject, but after determining that your keyword is *thoughtfulness*, you have discovered your focal point.

A precise example of the concentrating power of a keyword comes from a Canadian report studying how police investigated the disappearance of eighteen missing women in Vancouver, British Columbia.

A *Missing Women Commission of Inquiry* examined the response of police over a six year period, conducted 13 community forums, reviewed 385 written submissions, evaluated more than 200 exhibits, surveyed 20 other police forces, and produced a 1,400 page report containing 63 recommendations.

Commissioner Wally Oppal then communicated the full essence of the 4 volume, 500,000 word report in a single word: Forsaken. The missing women were forsaken by society and forsaken by police. The full title of the document is *Forsaken: The Report of the Missing Women Commission of Inquiry.*

A keyword is like a single grain of sand on a beach; but, in that single grain is a world of ideas.

"My term paper is almost finished. I updated my software, defragmented my hard drive, bookmarked an online dictionary, and installed new ink cartridges. Now all I need are some words and a topic!"

Here are four techniques for discovering your keyword:

1. Make A Keyword List
2. Consider Quotations
3. Create A Working Title
4. Deisgn A Poster

1. Make A Keyword List

Making a word list is the best technique for discovering your keyword.

Make two columns. In the first column write all the potential keywords related to your subject. Do not censor yourself.

When the first column is complete, write the opposites of your potential keywords in the second column. The list strategy works with all forms of writing and with any subject, goal, and audience.

Here is a partial keyword list for the subject *Wind Energy.*

Keyword List
Subject: Wind Energy

Possible Keywords	Opposites
wind farms	wind factories
present	past
more	less
conservation	waste
infinite	finite
jobs	unemployment
sailing	rowing
society	individuals
sustainable	unsustainable
corporations	cooperatives
taxes	private funding
benefits	costs
healthy	unhealthy
popular	unpopular
ecological footprint	environmental footprint
beautiful	ugly
support	blowback
survival	extinction
harvest	manufacture
controversy	agreement
replace	supplement
quiet	noisy
environmentally friendly	environmentally harmful
NIMBY (Not In My Backyard)	NIABY (Not In Anyone's Backyard)

Generating a list of twenty or thirty words with their opposites takes only a few minutes. Trust your instincts. Somewhere in the list lies your keyword. Try building your lists using single words, but do not be too hard on yourself. Sometimes you may need two or three words.

If your list of opposites contains some odd words, or words that are not exact opposites, that is normal. This is a creative exercise; all words are allowed. The list is for your eyes only, so do not hold back.

Listing keywords and keyword opposites focuses your thinking and often leads you in a new and rewarding direction. In the above example, the subject is wind energy. Wind farms come to mind. The opposite of a farm is a factory.

A farm is associated with a pastoral natural setting; a factory is aligned with a mechanized urban world. The first idea embraces the peaceful harvesting of electricity; the second thought involves the environmental and social costs of wind installations.

The keyword *present* and its opposite *past* suggests the idea of exploring what alternative energy looked like 25 or 50 years ago. The opposites *more* and *less* suggest writing about using less electricity instead of focusing on generating more. Contrasting *society* with *individuals* prompts comparing social needs with individual rights. And, *support* versus *blowback* raises the question of why some people are opposed to wind farms.

Building lists of words is quick and easy. Choosing your keyword from the list takes time and reflection. See what captures your intellect and your heart and consider what your research best supports.

Moving from, "My subject is wind energy" to "I am writing about blowback" focuses your writing and makes it more profound and memorable.

Diet books provide a perfect example of how a keyword steers writing. Every diet book has weight loss as its subject. But, as the keyword changes, the content and direction of the writing change profoundly.

Subject: Weight Loss

Keyword: Carbs
The Carb Lovers Diet: Eat What You Love, Get Slim For Life by Ellen Kunes
Eat carbs; get thin.

Keyword: Protein
The Dukan Diet: 2 Steps to Lose the Weight, 2 Steps to Keep It Off Forever by Pierre Dukan
Eat protein; avoid carbs.

Keyword: Blood Type
Eat Right 4 Your Type: The Individualized Diet Solution by Peter J. D'Adamo
First, consider your blood type.

Keyword: Brain
The Amen Solution: The Brain Healthy Way to Lose Weight and Keep It Off by Daniel G. Amen

"The first secret is that most weight problems occur between your ears."

Here is one last example. As you write a speech for a colleague's retirement dinner, a friend approaches and asks, "What are you writing about?" If you answer, "My subject is Jim's retirement," you have your subject. If you answer, "I am writing about friendship," or "I am writing about leadership," or " I am writing about loyalty," you have your keyword.

"Today, we celebrate Jim's retirement" becomes, "Today, we celebrate loyalty." From that point on, everything you say about Jim's retirement is controlled by one thing, the keyword *loyalty*.

2. Consider Quotations

Quotations provide another strategy for uncovering and confirming your keyword. Finding hundreds of quotations about your subject is as simple as searching the internet. For example, if you were writing about leadership, a search for *quotations about leadership* uncovers thousands of results:

> Innovation distinguishes between a leader and a follower. —Steve Jobs

> As we look ahead into the next century, leaders will be those who empower others. —Bill Gates

> Leadership has a harder job to do than just choose sides. It must bring sides together. —Jesse Jackson

> The key to successful leadership today is influence, not authority. —Kenneth Blanchard

Your subject is leadership, but you might discover that *innovation*, *empowerment*, *togetherness*, or *influence* is your keyword.

3. Create A Working Title

Before you settle into writing sentences and paragraphs, take your keyword for a test drive by using it in a title. Follow the example of authors who create a main title from their keyword and then compose a descriptive sub-title:

Abundance: The Future Is Better Than You Think by Peter H. Diamandis and Steven Kotler

Courage: Overcoming Fear and Igniting Self-Confidence by Debbie Ford

Heat: Adventures in the World's Most Firey Places by Bill Streever

Mastermind: How to Think Like Sherlock Holmes by Maria Konnikova

Willpower: Rediscovering the Greatest Human Strength by Roy F. Baumeister

Payback: Why We Retaliate, Redirect Aggression, and Take Revenge by David P. Barash and Judith Eve Lipto

Using the keyword list for wind turbines, here are some working titles:

Wind: Saving Ourselves One Revolution At A time

Timeless: The History of Wind Energy From Antiquity To The London Array

Blowback: Why Are People Rallying Against The Wind?

Sustainability: Infinite Resources In A Finite World

You might revise your title later, but for now it is an excellent test of your keyword.

Claudia Hammond: Writing a Title

Claudia Hammond is an award-winning broadcaster, writer, and psychology lecturer and the author of numerous articles and two books: *Emotional Rollercoaster* and *Time Warped*.

Time Warped took me two years to research and write, working approximately three days a week on it. It involved scanning the literature for time-related research in neuro-science, psychology and biology, but what made it harder was that within those subjects there are many different areas where time perception is studied, particularly within psychology. I also conducted approximately twenty interviews and many of the researchers I spoke to had no knowledge of the other areas I covered in the book, because in research terms they count as such different areas, often with very different time frames (everything from milliseconds to the way we hold the concept of centuries in mind).

I estimate that I read at least 200 different sources. Within psychology there was research from the fields of sensory perception, social psychology, cognitive psychology, psycholinguistics, animal behaviour and many others. It was when I thought about what tied all these findings together that I realised I wanted the title to convey the sense of the fluidity of time perception and the feeling that it tricks and surprises us. My editor and I came up with about fifty titles between us and we knew none of them was quite right. Then suddenly he emailed suggesting *Time Warped* and I knew instantly that was it.

If you can not create a working title, you may be wrestling with what you want to say. Take a break from your writing and let your subconscious do the work. Watch a movie.

4. Design A Poster

Thinking visually is another technique for generating and authenti-cating working titles.

Imagine that your essay, article, report, or after dinner speech is becoming a movie. Then, close your eyes and imagine what the poster for your movie looks like. When you wake from your nap, you might sketch a poster like this:

Set against a brilliant blue cloudless sky, pristine white

wind turbines tower over green rolling hills. A footprint appears. The title *Blowback* appears in large italic letters. The tagline on the poster reads *Even the wind leaves a footprint.*

A tagline on a movie poster is the equivalent of a subtitle on a written work. It is a pithy statement extending the meaning of the title.

Consider the poster for the movie *Braveheart*. Mel Gibson stares handsomely and defiantly into the distance. The tagline reads, "Every man dies, not every man really lives." The movie's title says that the main character has a brave heart. The tagline suggests that bravery has more to do with embracing life than facing death.

The poster for *Alien* portrays an extraterrestrial egg about to hatch a sinister monster. Directly beneath the eerie egg is the tagline, "In space no one can hear you scream." The tagline foreshadows a central theme in the movie: no one can hear you scream because we face our worst fears alone.

Taglines are often witty, sometimes philosophical, and generally clever. Here are several strategies for inventing taglines for an article, report, or essay on wind turbines.

1. Use Balanced Opposites

Annoy your neighbour; save the planet.
Instead of getting more, try using less.
Not in my backyard? Not in anyone's backyard!

2. Ask A Provocative Question

We have the knowledge, but do we have the wisdom?
Do the rights of the individual outweigh the needs of society?
What happens if we do nothing?

3. Work With Parallelism

Unnecessary. Unwanted. Uninvited.
No smog. No pollution. No problem.
Save your money. Save your children. Save yourself.

Sketch your movie poster. It does not matter if your drawing consists of stick men, a happy face, or birds resembling checkmarks. No one will see the poster unless you pin it on your wall.

Creating a poster fuels your creative engine and helps you further explore your keyword.

Chapter One Summary - Discover Your Keyword

Discover your keyword and develop a working title.

Keyword List
Subject: Canadian Identity

Possible Keywords	Opposites
snow	sand
ice	heat
polite	rude
peacekeeper	warmonger
cold	hot
eh	huh
RCMP	criminals
moose	cow
hockey	baseball
tolerance	intolerance
French	English
toque	hat
inventive	dull

Keyword: Cold

Quotation: *I don't trust any country that looks around a continent and says, "Hey, I'll take the frozen part." –* Jon Stewart

Working Title: Cold: What Is A Canadian?

Poster:

Print your keyword and working title on a piece of paper and put them on your fridge or bulletin board. As you write, keep asking yourself this question: How does this word, this sentence, this idea, relate to my keyword?

TWO
Determine Your Key Idea

Lord Ronald said nothing; he flung himself from the room, flung himself upon his horse and rode madly off in all directions.
– Stephen Leacock

The first secret of knowing what you want to say is uncovering your keyword. The second secret is determining your key idea.

Your mind is an infinite landscape full of information, examples, research, statistics, contradictions, arguments, opinions, and facts. You can ride madly off in all directions at once and not get lost because all of your ideas and all of the connections between your ideas exist in your mind simultaneously.

Readers, however, cannot navigate your mental landscape the way you do. They need a straight, well lit pathway headed in a single direction. This path is called your key idea, and it consists of two elements: a goal and a genre.

A goal is a reason for writing, your purpose. A genre is a framework for writing. In the same way we recognize musical genres such as Jazz, Classical, and Pop, we identify writing genres such as Comparison, Classification, and Definition.

Choosing a single goal focuses your writing and keeps you from writing madly off in all directions. Choosing a single genre organizes your writing because each genre offers a specific way of approaching your subject.

There are seven basic genres and countless goals. Before you put pen to paper, or fingertip to keyboard, determine your key idea by choosing and linking one goal with one genre:

    A. Identify Your Overall Goal

    B. Choose One Genre

    C. Link Your Goal And Genre

D. Understand The Conventions Of Your Genre

A. Identify Your Overall Goal

Capture your goal in a single action word.

Regardless of how complicated and sophisticated your objective is, express it in a single verb: my goal is arguing; my goal is proving; my goal is explaining; my goal is educating; my goal is describing.

Writers have many reasons for writing about a particular subject. Writing is energetic, full of action and life. Writers prove, compare, analyze, define, describe, discuss, review, teach, evaluate, classify, explore, report, persuade, and entertain. And that is the short list of a writer's goals.

However, focus on the overall purpose of the writing, the definitive goal.

When you write, "This report *proves* that being a vegetarian is healthier than being a vegan," you promise readers a solid argument supported by convincing evidence. Readers anticipate an argumentative point of view filled with facts, figures, and examples. Your primary goal is *proving* your point.

When you write, "This essay *compares* vegetarians and vegans," you promise a discussion of similarities and differences, not an argument. Readers expect a set of neutral, informative, and balanced observations.

Your goal is a promise, a contractual obligation.

B. Choose One Genre

Think of your genre as the framework for your writing, a way of organizing and presenting ideas.

Writers work with seven basic genres:

1. Sequencing
2. Comparison

3. Correlation
4. Classification
5. Debate
6. Definition
7. Observation

Each genre has a characteristic approach:

Genre	Approach
Sequencing	provide step-by-step instructions, explain how to, often the steps are numbered
Comparison	describe similarities and differences, explore advantages and disadvantages, discuss pros and cons
Correlation	explain causes and effects, describe links between events, establish direct relationships, examine potential relationships
Classification	systematically categorize items, make lists, label, describe
Debate	take a stance for or against, question and challenge ideas, make a case, argue
Definition	delineate the meaning of a word or a concept, present a comprehensive and extended characterization
Observation	describe, appeal to the senses, personalize, tell a story, paint a picture, collect and synthesise information

Each genre has a recognizable look and feel:

Genre	Look and Feel
Sequencing	*How To Remember Names – Five Easy Tricks* by Erin Matlock In the first of a two part series, let's look at five tricks to better remember names. 1) Pay Attention
Comparison	*A Cost Comparison of Home Brew Vs. Store-Bought Beer* by Julia Scott Well, I finally decided to settle the debate once and for all. Here is my breakdown of home brew vs. store-bought beer.

Genre	Look and Feel
Correlation	*9 Reasons Golf Is Good For Your Brain* by Erin Matlock No matter what your handicap, golf can provide a fun, social way to stimulate your brain, increase your self esteem and sharpen your concentration. Here's how.
Classification	*The Three Types of Computer User* by Stuart Sierra I think nearly all computer users can be divided into three broad categories based on the way they think about computers.
Debate	*Food and Wine Pairing is Just a Big Scam* by Alder Yarrow [W]ine drinkers around the world, you've been hoodwinked. Tricked. Bamboozled. Conned. Before you throw that glass at your monitor, let me explain.
Definition	*What Is Forgiveness?* by Hollye Dexter What exactly is forgiveness? Is it condoning the other person's behavior? Denying your own pain so another person can feel better? . . . I think it is much more complex than that.
Observation	*The Plight Of Younger Workers* by Francis Fong Two weeks ago, TD Economics released a brief report . . . highlighting the surge in job creation among Canadians over 60 years of age during the recession and subsequent recovery. In this report, we chronicle the fortunes of those at the opposite end of the age spectrum (those aged 15-24 years).

Because each genre has distinctive qualities, choosing a single genre helps you clarify and organize your message. Will you explain how to make friends, argue that friends are more important than family, or describe three kinds of friends?

The names of genres also name writing strategies. For example, any document can contain comparison, observation, or classification. Opening an essay with a definition is a common strategy. But these strategies do not define the global genre. The overall approach does.

Although writers use many strategies within a given genre, taken as a whole, readers recognize the writing as belonging to a particular genre. Sometimes, all it takes is the title:

Genre	Title
Sequencing	*How to Spot An Untrustworthy Smile*
Comparison	*Social Versus Financial Thinking*
Correlation	*Why Loud Music In Bars Increases Alcohol Consumption*
Classification	*Six Types Of Play*
Debate	*Why Psychology Is Not Just Common Sense*
Definition	*What Is Happiness?*
Observation	*How Memory Works: 10 Things Most People Get Wrong*
All titles are by Jeremy Dean at PsyBlog spring.org.uk.	

C. Link Your Goal And Genre

Match your goal with a genre. Here are some common pairings:

Genre	Goal
Sequencing	teach, explain, guide, coach, describe a process
Comparison	compare, evaluate, prove, describe, review
Correlation	connect, analyze, argue, prove, describe, investigate
Classification	categorize, list, describe, differentiate, observe
Debate	argue, refute, question, disagree, dispute
Definition	set limits, distinguish, examine, characterize
Observation	describe, summarize, illustrate, recreate, investigate

Always link your goal and genre by articulating their relationship. In the following examples, the goal is italicized and the genre is underlined.

This blog *teaches* you how to post a tweet <u>by providing a step by step set of instructions</u>.

This article *explains* why winter tires are safer on ice than all season tires <u>by comparing</u> traction, control, and stopping distances.

This report <u>analyzes the effects</u> of talking on a cell phone while driving and *argues* in favour of higher fines for distracted driving.

This essay *describes* three types of neurons <u>by classifying</u> them according to function.

This editorial *contradicts* popular opinion <u>by arguing</u> that high salaries do not necessarily attract competent managers.

This memo *limits* activities at office parties <u>by defining</u> acceptable and unacceptable behaviour.

This history *recreates* life in seventeenth century England <u>by describing</u> the life of a baker.

Avoid confusing your goal with your genre. For example, do not write, "This essay *compares* solar and wind power" when you mean, "This essay *proves* that wind power is better than solar power <u>by comparing</u> them.

Exploring all seven genres is an excellent strategy for considering, and reconsidering, your key message and your basic goal. It also helps you separate your genre from your goal.

In the following example, education is the subject and the keyword is homeschooling. The writer is interested in the trend of homeschooling, but has not settled on a specific goal. By taking each genre for a test drive, goals become apparent. The goal is italicized and the genre is underlined.

Subject: Education
Keyword: Homeschooling

Genre	Working Title
Sequencing	Homeschooling: How To Get Started This web page *explains* how to get started homeschooling your children <u>by providing a step-by-step guide</u> for planning and delivering a grade one curriculum.
Comparison	Homeschooling Versus Public Schooling This article *discusses the pros and cons* of homeschooling <u>by comparing</u> student outcomes in three categories: social development, standardized test scores, and continuing education.

Genre	Working Title
Correlation	Why Do Some Parents Choose Homeschooling? This essay *explores* <u>three reasons why</u> some parents choose homeschooling: religious concerns, curriculum control, role modelling.
Classification	Homeschooling: Three Styles Of Teaching This blog *describes* three styles of teaching used by homeschooling parents <u>by classifying them</u> as coaches, taskmasters, or freethinkers.
Debate	Why Homeschooling Is A Bad Idea This editorial *discourages* homeschooling <u>by arguing</u> that few parents are competent teachers.
Definition	What Is Homeschooling? This article *defines* the term homeschooling <u>by describing</u> the nature, challenges, and rewards of this growing movement.
Observation	Homeschooling: Merlin The Mathematician Merlin is the only person I know who can find the square root of a number without using a calculator. He is well-read, well-spoken, and well-educated. And he is homeschooled.

D. Understand The Conventions Of Your Genre

Understanding the conventions of a written genre does not restrict writers any more than understanding the conventions of a musical genre limits musicians. As Shepherd and Watters wrote in *The Evolution of Cybergenres*, the concept of genre "allows us to recognize items that are similar even in the midst of great diversity. For instance, the detective novel is a particular genre and we are able to recognize novels as members of that genre, even though the novels themselves may be very different."

There are no rules for matching genres and goals. Some very creative writing comes from inventive pairings. But readers have basic expectations for each genre. The remainder of this chapter describes the conventions of the seven basic genres.

1. Sequencing

Defining Characteristic: Explains a step by step procedure

Readers Expect: A sequential list of instructions or events

Generic Title: How To Control Stress Through Deep Breathing

The sequencing genre, also referred to as the *how to* genre, is popular. Dale Carnegie's *How To Win Friends And Influence People* has sold more than 15 million copies. Published in 1936, it is still in print today and now available as an eBook.

If your goal is writing a book, article, blog, or manual that teaches how to do something, include the phrase "how to" in your title and provide a sequential list of the steps. Number the steps if appropriate.

How To Remember Things by Dr. Alex Lickerman

> The mind's capacity to store and recall information is truly wondrous. . . . Though much of what follows are techniques I used to survive my first two years of medical school, much of the science that proves they work is new.
>
> 1. Become interested in what you're learning.
>
> 2. Find a way to leverage your visual memory.
>
> 3. Create a mental memory tree.
>
> 4. Associate what you're trying to learn with what you already know.
>
> 5. Write out items to be memorized over and over and over. . . .

A variation on this approach involves a theoretical, rather than a practical, explanation of how to achieve a goal. Articles like *How To Win The War On Drugs*, *The Challenge for Green Energy: How to Store Excess Electricity*, and *How To Stop Crime* do not provide a numbered step by step set of instructions. They are more of a discussion of sequential possibilities and less of a manual.

Although the approach is straightforward, the creative possibilities and range of topics are infinite.

How to Write a Bad Resume by Elaine Basham and Sue Sarkesian

So, I've decided to put together a list of just a few of the things that make for a really bad resume. By avoiding these pitfalls, you might improve your odds of getting in the door for an interview. Then it's up to you to seal the deal.

1. Focusing on responsibilities, not achievements.

2. Putting anything in your resume that you might have to back-peddle from in an interview.

3. Using acronyms like alphabet soup.

However, before saying the opposite of what you mean, identify and respect your audience's expectations. Not everyone expects or understands satire and sarcasm. An after dinner speech ironically entitled *How To Increase Global Warming* might be taken literally and alienate some people. Sophisticated irony that works well with one audience may fail miserably with another.

Consider the following paragraph by Emma Teitel. Is she being playfully ironic or deadly serious?

Emma Teitel: Writing Conclusions

Emma Teitel is an award winning columnist featured in Canada's national current affairs magazine *Maclean's*. Along with her work as a writer, she is also a public speaker. twitter.com/ EmmaRoseTeitel

When I write conclusions I do everything my English teacher told me not to: My sentences begin with and. And but. I don't restate my thesis. I write a new one. I make sure to leave my most interesting argument for the very end, and (unless the piece is about something very sad and serious) I try to finish with a joke. If you've just completed high school you may be under the impression that essays should take the "five paragraph hamburger" form, in which the bottom bun signifies the intro, the burger and condiments signify the body, and the top bun signifies the conclusion. The problem with this model is that the bun is the worst part of the burger, and your conclusion should be the very best part of your piece. So scrap the burger model, write down what you believe is your most interesting and surprising argument, and save the best for last.

2. Comparison

Defining Characteristic: Describes similarities and differences

Readers Expect: An ordered and balanced discussion and an evaluation

Generic Title: Women and Men Manage Stress Differently

Comparison is also known as compare and contrast. Writers invariably announce the comparison genre in their titles:

Comparing Written And Oral Approaches To Clinical Reporting In Nursing by Diana Johnson Jefferies et al.

Comparing The Ethical Attitudes Of Business And Criminal Justice Students by Lydia Segal et al.

Comparing Cars—Environmental And Cost Concerns by Edward J. Lazaros

Comparing Democratic Maturity Test Scores For German And American College Freshman by Rosemarie Kolstad et al.

Comparison is always based on points of comparison. In his article, *Tablet Vs Ereader—Which Is Better For You,* Jared Scott uses six points of comparison:

1. Functionality
2. Price
3. Screen
4. Battery Life
5. Size and Weight
6. eBook Selection

Similarly, in *The Canadian And American Health Care Systems*, Madore uses four points of comparison:

1. Access to Health Care Services
2. Financial Barriers to Care
3. Extent of Benefits
4. Administration

When your goal is comparing A and B, choose from one of two frameworks:

1. Alternate your comparison of A and B point by point:
   A-B, A-B

2. Write a series of observations only about A. Then
   write a series of observations only about B: A-A-A,
   B-B-B.

The following example uses the A-B, A-B, A-B model and three points
of comparison:

One If By Land, Two If By Sea: Cruising Versus All Inclusive

Should you cruise or stay at an all inclusive resort? Which
is the better deal? We did the research and here is what
we found in terms of food, drink, and entertainment.

Food
On a cruise ship, the dining is both plentiful and
exquisite. Cruise ships pride themselves, and rightly so,
on the quality, quantity, and variety of their culinary
delights. From buffet to banquet to 24 hour room service,
the selection, service, and quality are five star.

All inclusive resorts cater less to epicures. Generally
speaking, the meals are fine but unremarkable. Some,
but not all, suites include 24 hour room service, and the
selection is often not as varied or as accessible as it is on
board a cruise ship.

Drink
Cruise ship fares do not include alcohol. Some cruise
lines charge for milk and pop. Cruisers are, after all, a
captive audience. If you like coffee, tea, and fruit juice, no
problem. And do not even think about sneaking alcohol
onboard. It will not make it.

Often, all inclusive packages include drinks. However,
the beer, wine, and liquor may be restricted to domestic
brands. You may pay extra if you are a connoisseur.

Entertainment
Cruise ships book first rate entertainment that includes Broadway musicals, live orchestras, original productions, comedians, dancers, jugglers, acrobats, magicians, and more. The entertainers are world class.

Entertainment at an all inclusive is more subdued. Entertainers are typically local performers. They are professionals and more than competent, but they are not the A-list performers you find on a cruise ship.

Adopt the A-A-A, B-B-B model, and the same review looks like this:

One If By Land, Two If By Sea: Cruising Versus All Inclusive

Food, Drink, and Entertainment On A Cruise Ship
On a cruise ship, the dining is both plentiful and exquisite. Cruise ships pride themselves, and rightly so, on the quality, quantity, and variety of their culinary delights. From buffet to banquet to 24 hour room service, the selection, service, and quality are five star.

Cruise ship fares do not include alcohol. Some cruise lines charge for milk and pop. Cruisers are, after all, a captive audience. If you like coffee, tea, and fruit juice, no problem. And do not even think about sneaking alcohol onboard. It will not make it.

Cruise ships book first rate entertainment that includes Broadway musicals, live orchestras, original productions, comedians, dancers, jugglers, acrobats, magicians, and more. The entertainers are world class.

Food, Drink, and Entertainment At An All Inclusive Resort
All inclusive resorts cater less to epicures. Generally speaking, the meals are fine but unremarkable. Some, but not all, suites include 24 hour room service, and the selection is often not as varied or as accessible as it is

on board a cruise ship.

Often, all inclusive packages include drinks. However, the beer, wine, and liquor may be restricted to domestic brands. You may pay extra if you are a connoisseur.

Entertainment at an all inclusive is more subdued. Entertainers are typically local performers. They are professionals and more than competent, but they are not the A-list performers you find on a cruise ship.

Both patterns work. But the A B, A B, A B method highlights similarities and differences more immediately and dramatically by placing points of comparison side by side. When the comparison is compartmentalized, the reader must remember what was said five or six paragraphs earlier.

Another disadvantage of the compartmentalized mode is the trap of introducing a point of comparison in section A but leaving it out in section B. When comparing points side by side, this error is less likely.

Writers use comparison for proving a point, making a recommendation, discussing pros and cons, highlighting similarities and differences, and evaluating. But, comparison may be neutral or simply descriptive. Writing about Viceroy and Monarch butterflies, one author compares them on the basis of scientific names, appearance, diet, and size and simply concludes minor differences exist between the species.

3. Correlation

Defining Characteristic: Discusses causes and effects

Readers Expect: Evidence that a relationship exists or may exist

Generic Title: The Two Leading Causes of Stress: Money and Work

The title often signals the correlation genre:

Why Do We Smoke Cigarettes by Erenst Dichter

What Does Smoking Tobacco Do to Your Body? by David Carnes

First, decide if you will explore causes, effects, or both causes and effects:

Studying the Causes of Recent Climate Change by Benjamin Santer

Effects of Climate Change on Fishery Species in Florida by Jonathan M. Shenker

The Causes and Effects of Global Warming by David G. Victor

Second, decide if there is sufficient and convincing evidence that establishes a connection between two events. Account for as many variables as possible.

For example, assuming a direct connection between smaller class size and improved student outcomes seems reasonable. However, as Pedder points out, many factors affect student performance.

Are Small Classes Better? Understanding Relationships between Class Size, Classroom Processes and Pupils' Learning by David Pedder

> Politicians are rightly told that the messages from the substantial body of research evidence on class size are ambiguous and inconsistent. Neither the large-scale class size experiments . . . nor the statistical syntheses of all relevant class size studies . . . nor the reanalyses of the influential Tennessee experimental study . . . provide clear support for the claim that class size is an important determinant of pupil achievement.

Similarly, arguing that lower tuition fees lead to higher university enrolments seems prudent. However, writing for the Montreal Economic Institute, Kozhaya and Belzile present a different cause effect relationship.

Would Higher Tuition Fees Restrict Access To University Studies? by Norma Kozhaya and Germain Belzile

In reality, this debate is based on a false choice. The available data for the various Canadian provinces show no direct relationship between tuition fee levels and access to university studies. In other words, low tuition fees do not result in high enrolments.

Third, in terms of cause and effect, consider which came first, the chicken or the egg. For example, does marijuana use lead to academic problems, or do academic problems lead to marijuana use?

Marijuana Use at School and Achievement-Linked Behaviors by Kristin V. Finn

The direction of the relationship between marijuana use and school behavior is unclear. Some research has found that marijuana use results in subsequent academic problems (Fergusson, Horwood, & Beautrais, 2003); but in Hawkins, Catalano, and Miller's (1992) review of research, many of these same academic problems were portrayed as risk factors for drug use. In either case, the research consistently demonstrates an inverse relationship between general marijuana use and school success.

4. Classification

Defining Characteristic: Sorts and describes by type

Readers Expect: Categories, lists, and descriptions

Generic Title: Five Types of Stress

The classification genre compartmentalizes by type: There are *Seven Types of Ambiguity, Six Types Of Nutrients, Five Branches of Chemistry, Four Kinds of Love, and Three Types of Irony.*

Classification divides ideas, events, and objects into categories, labels them, and describes them. When you classify, first specify a specific number of categories: three types of computer users, six kinds of snow, twelve styles of dancing. Second, describe each category in the order listed.

Wordplay

There are three types of wordplay: the pun, the one-liner, the comeback.

First there is the pun. . . .

The one-liner comes second. . . .

Third in line is the comeback. . . .

Stick with your number. If you declare there are three types of wordplay, do not wander down a path that leads to a brief discussion of a fourth type.

Carve your categories from the same block of wood. The pun, the one-liner, and the comeback are all types of wordplay. But the pun, the one-liner, and the comedian are not part of the same group.

Spend the same amount of time describing each group. For example, Sierra identifies three types of computer users and dedicates a single paragraph to each type:

The Three Types of Computer User by Stuart Sierra

I think nearly all computer users can be divided into three broad categories based on the way they think about computers.

The vast majority of computer users are application-oriented. They have training and experience exclusively with commercial software. They understand concepts peculiar to computers such as files, folders, saving, and deleting. . . .

The second largest group consists of goal-oriented users. These users focus exclusively on the goals they want to accomplish and neither understand nor care about the software they use to accomplish those goals. . . .

The third and smallest group of computer users — ironically, the original computer users — is comprised of hackers. Hackers are computer-oriented computer users. They have learned how to think like a computer, to understand the processes the computer goes through....

Similarly, in *What Kind of Blogger Are You?* Peric develops and describes seven groups; each grouping receives equal time. Peric also employs the organizational technique of creating subcategories. Under each of her category headings, she includes a quotation and a list of tags. This makes her writing unified, organized, and thoughtful. Here is a sample.

What Kind of Blogger Are You? 7 Different Blogger Types Explained by Eva Percic

No blogger is the same. Every blog we read from our users has something unique and different: it might be a name, an unusual writing style, great photos, or an extraordinary topic. Uniqueness makes a blog interesting or actually, the person behind it does.

7 different blogger types:

Hedonists: "I blog about life in general and its enjoyments."

Hedonists promote different lifestyles to enrich people's daily routines. They are emotional and are not afraid to express feelings or reach out to others.

Tags: food, travel, sex, shopping, life, entertainment

Techies: "I'm fascinated by new technologies and their applications to various personal and professional fields."

Techies don't get much satisfaction from the writing process, but enjoy spreading their word, sharing knowledge and educating.

Tags: IT, gaming

Professionals: "Blogging is part of my job."

Professionals present accomplishments and seek feedback from their followers. For them, blogging is all about making connections.

Tags: corporate, consultants, belletristics, copywriters

5. Debate

Defining Characteristic: Argues a point of view

Readers Expect: Valid and substantial evidence

Generic Title: Stress! It Only Exists In Your Mind

Use the argument genre for debating and editorializing.

A Planet for the Taking by David Suzuki

Canadians live under the remarkable illusion that we are technologically advanced people. Everything around us denies that assumption.

A Problem With Wind Power by Eric Rosenbloom

A little research, however, reveals that wind power does not in fact live up to the claims made by its advocates (see part I), that its impact on the environment and people's lives is far from benign (see part II), and that with such a poor record and prospect the money spent on it could be much more effectively directed (see part III).

The convention of this genre is the presentation of mountains of evidence and an assertive tone. Writers employ facts, statistics, examples, quotations, charts, tables, illustrations, comparisons, definitions, and descriptions and write with conviction.

In his book, *You Are Not So Smart: Why You Have Too Many Friends on Facebook, Why Your Memory Is Mostly Fiction, and 46 Other Ways*

You're Deluding Yourself, David McRaney argues that sometimes, because of our expectations, we cannot tell good wine from bad.

Knowing he faces an uphill battle in converting wine aficionados to his viewpoint, McRaney piles on the evidence. First he cites a French 2001 study showing that wine experts could not distinguish between expensive and cheap wine; then he describes another study demonstrating that wine experts could not tell the difference between red wine and white wine.

Next he offers evidence from a 2008 Cal-Tech experiment that "put the tasters in a brain scanner." Researchers found that when subjects were told they were drinking a $90 bottle of wine, they praised it, and a specific region in the brain lit up. When the identical bottle of wine was presented as being worth $10, they gave it a poor rating and the brain region did not light up.

When debating, you not only prove your case, you disprove the defence.

For example, in 2008 Enbridge began public consultation on a proposed $5.5 billion pipeline project that would see twin buried pipelines traverse northern Alberta and BC. The 1,177 km pipeline would transport oil from Bruderheim, Alberta to Kitimat, British Columbia at a rate of 525,000 barrels a day.

A fiery public debate followed. Note how each side methodically presents facts and figures supporting their arguments.

Enbridge Northern Gateway Pipelines by Enbridge

> We've worked hard to ensure that the project will create a lasting legacy of local investment, tax revenue, and jobs for the North. . . .

> • About 1,150 long-term job opportunities throughout the Canadian economy, including 104 permanent operating positions created with Northern Gateway and 113 positions with the associated marine services

- About 62,700 person-years of employment will be created throughout the Canadian economy during the construction phase of the project, with 3,000 direct on-site workers required during the peak period of construction

Enbridge Pipe Dreams and Nightmares by Marc Lee

Projections of large employment gains are based on models that greatly exaggerate actual job creation, and are stated in "person-years" of employment. In reality, total job creation from pipeline construction will be small relative to the economies of BC and Alberta and existing employment:

- Together, construction and pipe manufacture amount to no more than 8,600 person-years of employment — only about 14% of the 63,000 person-years estimated by the modeling.

Enbridge's modeling exercise makes a number of implausible assumptions. In particular, it assumes that workers would otherwise be unemployed; yet, current labour shortages imply that the vast majority of workers would be employed elsewhere if the NGP does not go forward.

Once built, pipeline operations would support a total of 217 permanent jobs. Enbridge's larger public claim of 1,146 total jobs per year is derived from modeling that suffers from the same shortcomings as noted for construction jobs, including a very large share (37% of the total) coming from induced employment.

Enbridge Northern Gateway Pipelines by Enbridge

As part of Northern Gateway's planning, a team of over 200 environmental experts and scientists conducted comprehensive marine biology, geology, archaeology and other environmental analysis along the project route.

Pipelines are the safest method of transporting fuels, as they have the least amount of releases of any transportation mode. . . . On average, for every barrel of oil (42 gallons) shipped 1,000 miles, less than one teaspoon is lost from a liquid pipeline.

Enbridge Pipe Dreams and Nightmares by Marc Lee

Available evidence suggests that oil spills are quite common and a cost of doing business. For example, a 35-mile stretch of the Kalamazoo River in Michigan has been closed since July 2010, when 843,000 gallons of oil leaked from another Enbridge pipeline, which was transporting oil sands crude, with an estimated clean-up cost of $500 million. But this is far from an isolated incident. An investigative report from the New York Times in the wake of that spill found that: "Since 1990, more than 5,600 incidents were reported involving land-based hazardous liquid pipelines, releasing a total of more than 110 million gallons of mostly crude and petroleum products."

The US Office on Pipeline Safety reports statistics on pipeline spills, safety and property damage, although statistics on-line only go from 1986 to 2003. During that timeframe, 3,300 incidents led to more than 125 million gallons spilled, of which 76 million was recovered. These incidents led to a total of $857 million in property damage, and 291 injuries and deaths. A corporate profile by the Polaris Institute notes that Enbridge is no exception when it comes to pipeline spills. Between 1999 and 2010, Enbridge pipelines experienced 804 spills, with the release of 168,645 barrels, or 26.8 million litres, of hydrocarbons into the environment.

Winning a debate depends heavily on the persuasiveness of your evidence. Hearsay, common knowledge, undocumented statements, and personal opinion are not as convincing as well-documented facts and figures:

The Problem with Education Funding

> Let us not forget that, over time, the quality of education in Canada has been eroded. I don't have specific evidence of this, but ask anyone who is going to be truthful and they will agree.

Free University Education Is Long Overdue In Canada

> Everyone knows that free education leads to a better educated citizenry and better access to education.

Lowering Fees Does Not Make Universities More Accessible by Norma Kozhaya

> In 2003-04, average undergraduate tuition fees in Quebec were $1,862 a year, the lowest in Canada and more than $2,000 less than the Canadian average of $4,025.
>
> But Quebec has one of Canada's lower university enrolment rates, with just 20 per cent of its 20-to-21-year-olds registered full time at university in 2000. On the other hand, Nova Scotia, which has the highest tuition fees at $5,557, also had the highest enrolment rate at 32.6 per cent.
>
> University enrolment rates have actually declined slightly in Quebec in spite of the tuition freeze that has been in effect since 1994, while enrolments in Ontario have increased, despite major tuition fee increases that brought fees this year to $4,923.

6. Definition

Defining Characteristic: Isolates a word

Readers Expect: A thorough and extended discussion of the meaning of a word

Generic Title: What Is Stress?

Writers use the definition genre for exploring in detail the meaning of a word. The entire composition is devoted to this exploration.

Toward a Definition of Multiculturalism by Caleb Rosado

> It is an axiom of our times that our world is rapidly changing. With change comes not only a different view of the world, but also changes in language to name that "new" world. Old words take on new meanings and new words enter the vocabulary, resulting in another way of "seeing."
>
> . . . .
>
> The purpose of this article is to provide an operational definition of multiculturalism and its value for all groups as a basis for understanding the changes coming to our society.

What is Forgiveness? by Hollye Dexter

> What exactly is forgiveness? Is it condoning the other person's behavior? Denying your own pain so another person can feel better? Letting another off the hook, and then carrying their shame for them? Is it as simple as letting go of a balloon that floats away into the atmosphere? I think it is much more complex than that.

On Defining Music by Stephen Davies

> In this paper I reflect on the enterprise of defining music. Although I critically review some proposed

definitions in order to show the difficulties inherent in the task, I do not offer a counter definition. Instead, I consider four strategies that might be adopted by the would-be definer. I argue that none of these alone can succeed, though, in combination, they might.

What Is Guilt? by Simona Rich

Guilt is a natural emotion that comes as a result of the person doing something that is against his or her values.

It is like a built-in self-correction system that notifies you the second you get out of harmony with what you consider right or wrong.

7. Observation

Defining Characteristic: Describes

Readers Expect: A personal or an objective report

Generic Title: A Day In The Life Of A Stressed Out Mom

The observation genre is often a first person narrative:

The Peace: An Exploration in Photographs by Donald A. Pettit

Wildness lives in neglected corners of backyards, in special spots hidden in urban parks, or untrammelled places, free from human mark. The Peace is a generous landscape, bountiful in all of these, but especially the wildest kind of wild.

This is where I most like to be. The camera that takes me there is both reason and method. Looking out through the lens, moving with decisions of composition, viewpoint, and exposure, I look inside too, for relationships, insight, and mood. Photographs are bits of these, crystallized.

Observation is also commonly third person narrative:

How Do You Fight City Hall (And Everyone Else)?

> The surveyors were first on the scene. They left innocuous little stakes in the ground with fluorescent orange bows tied to them hardly a portent of things to come. Then came the earth movers, the graders, the cats, and the trucks: flat deck trucks, gravel trucks, water trucks, pump trucks, and vac trucks, trucks carrying rigs and chemicals and camps.

Observation ranges from the practical to the poetic. It can be neutral or emotional. Note in the following example how the language changes from descriptive to emotive: *water* becomes *heavily polluted water*, a *mix of water, sand, and various chemicals* becomes *radioactive elements and toxic metals like arsenic*, and *wastewater* becomes *chemicals stored at the well site pollute the air.*

Fracking: The Process (cleanwater.org)

> Fracking - also called hydro-fracking or, officially, horizontal drilling coupled with multi-stage hydraulic fracturing - is a relatively new process of natural gas extraction. Here's a step-by-step look:
>
> 1. A well is drilled vertically to the desired depth, then turns ninety degrees and continues horizontally for several thousand feet into the shale believed to contain the trapped natural gas.
>
> 2. A mix of water, sand, and various chemicals is pumped into the well at high pressure in order to create fissures in the shale through which the gas can escape.
>
> 3. Natural gas escapes through the fissures and is drawn back up the well to the surface, where it is processed, refined, and shipped to market.
>
> 4. Wastewater (also called "flowback water" or

"produced water") returns to the surface after the fracking process is completed. In Michigan, this water is contained in steel tanks until it can be stored long-term by deep injection in oil and gas waste wells.

. . . .

Gas wells that are fracked are very different from traditional natural gas wells. They are bigger, deeper, and present a host of environmental threats:

- They require two to four million gallons of fresh water per well, which could de-water nearby streams or rivers, particularly during droughts like the one that is now endangering Texas.

- They produce a million or more gallons per well of heavily polluted water which must be properly treated and disposed of. This water is very salty—6 to 10 times saltier than the ocean—and also contains radioactive elements and toxic metals like arsenic that it picks up from the earth. In 2008, drinking water consumers along the Monongahela River in Pennsylvania were warned not to use the water because it was too polluted, in part from discharges of water from Marcellus shale wells.

- The wells require exceptionally large well pads—up to 5 acres each—and a series of roads and pipelines to connect them. These pads, roads and pipelines often run through pristine areas, damaging streams and fragmenting our forest habitat.

- The chemicals stored at the well site pollute the air; and the thousands of diesel truck trips needed for each well spew soot into the air. Diesel soot has been linked to variety of cardiovascular diseases, including lung cancer.

Chapter Two Summary - Choose A Genre And A Goal

Choose a genre, focus on a single goal, and link your genre and goal.

Subject: Canadian Identity

Keyword: Cold

Working Title: Cold: What Is A Canadian?

Genre: Definition

Link: This essay <u>defines</u> what a Canadian is by *describing* three choices that Canadians make: our choice of sports arenas, our choice of real estate, and our choice of pastimes.

Place your goal and genre next to your keyword. As you write, ask yourself this: Am I following a single path or writing off in all directions at once?

THREE
Understand Your Audience

You were a perfect success: the audience was a dismal failure.
– George Bernard Shaw

Knowing what you want to say becomes increasingly apparent as you understand and acknowledge your audience's expectations, interests, opinions, abilities, and background.

As you explore your key word and key idea, remain true to yourself. Write from your heart. But understand and respect your audience. Preparing to host the Academy Awards, Hollywood's most ceremonious and serious awards show, Seth McFarlane, creator and head writer of the unceremonious and satirical television series *Family Guy*, acknowledged the importance of maintaining a balance between respect and integrity:

> It's a very specific ceremony with a very specific tone.
> The challenge will be to keep it funny, keep it lively, and
> stay true to what it is I do.

This chapter presents three strategies for shaping your message by understanding your audience:

1. Make The Audience Real

2. Acknowledge Their Point Of View

3. Speak Their Language

Bruce Ravelli: Audience

Dr. Bruce Ravelli is the co-author of *Exploring Sociology* and *Sociology for Everyone* as well as numerous articles.

Most of my writing is for students. To try and make my writing connect with the student, I force myself to see them as visitors to my country. I actively take on the role of tour guide who has the pleasure of showing my guests the very best of my discipline in the hopes that they will want to come back. Positioning myself in this way helps me achieve my personal commitment to never alienate or exclude anyone but rather to entice and inspire all of them.

---

1. Make The Audience Real

An author writing a book about time management who says, "I am writing for busy people" probably winds up saying, "I know what I want to say; I just don't know how to say it."

However, the book's content becomes clearer when the statement becomes, "I am writing for Jane who is a single working mom holding down two part time jobs and taking correspondence courses."

Make your audience real. Picture their lives; empathize with them; visualize them.

Instead of saying, "I am writing for my Sociology professor," try this: "I am writing for Dr. Haugen who has a great sense of humour, an extensive vocabulary, and a keen interest in contemporary First Nations issues."

Consider the difference between these two statements:

I am writing a speech for the Polar Bear Club.

Versus

I am writing a speech for a group of middle aged men who just ate a questionable dinner and are now sitting on uncomfortable chairs in an overheated, stuffy conference room waiting for my talk about panning for gold in Alaska.

If you are writing a family history, imagine your book being read by other authors or by a historian 500 years from now. Your audience might be larger than you think.

If you are writing an essay for a grade, imagine your instructor at home, late Sunday night, exhausted from a weekend at the library, slugging through forty-five essays that all begin exactly the same way: "Webster's dictionary defines bulimia as. . . ." Your audience might be ready for something new.

Do not write for a generic audience. Write for people who have lives and minds of their own.

2. Acknowledge Their Point Of View

Shaping your message depends in part on whether your audience is welcoming or unreceptive.

If your message is controversial and your audience is hostile, let them know you recognize their point of view even as you present yours.

Communicating an unpopular message depends on acknowledging and respecting the beliefs and opinions and of your readers:

The Other Difference Between Boys and Girls by Richard M. Restak

> Boys think differently from girls. . . . I know how offensive
> that will sound to feminists and others. . . . As the father
> of three daughters, I am well aware of the discrimination

girls suffer. But social equality for men and women really depends on recognizing these differences in brain behavior.

Against the Wind: Taking the Opposition Head On by Wayne Gulden

This web site is in the unenviable position of being a messenger of bad news about wind energy. And wind energy was, at least intuitively, so promising! Most of us know we can't keep doing what we're doing – burning through all the fossil fuels we can find – and wind seems to promise a carbon-free, inexhaustible and benign source that doesn't send money overseas.

As much as all of us, including myself, would want this rosy picture to be true, the actual evidence so far paints a far different picture. I understand that many people will resist hearing this bad news, preferring to label me a NIMBY, a Luddite, unscientific, oil-industry-loving, climate-change-denying, jealous – anything to dismiss me. I'm sorry to disappoint, but I'm simply someone who thinks evidence is a better guide to reality than wishful thinking. And the existing evidence says to me that wind energy has no redeeming value while its downsides are substantial.

Food and Wine Pairing Is Just A Big Scam by Alder Yarrow

Did I just say that? Yes I did. And increasingly I'm hearing it from wine professionals that I know — spoken, of course, in hushed tones and off the record. Most professional sommeliers and wine writers wouldn't be caught dead uttering such terms in public, let alone publishing them. So I guess it's up to us bloggers to spread the word: wine drinkers around the world, you've been hoodwinked. Tricked. Bamboozled. Conned.

Before you throw that glass at your monitor, let me explain.

Being understood comes from understanding. The more you identify with your audience, the clearer your message becomes:

The Gap: Minimum Wage and Executive Compensation

> In 2012, the Chairman and Chief Executive Officer of The Walt Disney Company earned $3,352,320.66 a month. Assuming a forty hour work week, that is $20,952.00 an hour. Honest. It seems like a mistake, but the decimal and commas are in the right places. According to the company's SEC filings and *Notice of 2013 Annual Meeting and Proxy Statement*, the CEO earned $40,227,848.00 in executive compensation in 2012 representing a $6.7 million dollar raise from the previous year.

3. Speak Their Language

Writing is like joining an ongoing conversation: before participating, listen. Gain a sense of how people think, talk, and write in your field. Read what they read.

Speak their language and communicate with your audience by understanding their vocabulary, conventions, concerns, and expectations. Note how NASA produces different versions of a document for different audiences:

Audience: Grades K TO 4

> Pluto was discovered in 1930 by an astronomer from the United States. An astronomer is a person who studies stars and other objects in space.

> Pluto was known as the smallest planet in the solar system and the ninth planet from the sun.

Audience: Higher Education

> Discovered in 1930, Pluto was long considered our

solar system's ninth planet. But after the discovery of similar intriguing worlds deeper in the distant Kuiper Belt, icy Pluto was reclassified as a dwarf planet. This new class of worlds may offer some of the best evidence about the origins of our solar system. Pluto is also a member of a group of objects that orbit in a disc-like zone beyond the orbit of Neptune called the Kuiper Belt. This distant realm is populated with thousands of miniature icy worlds, which formed early in the history of our solar system. These icy, rocky bodies are called Kuiper Belt objects or transneptunian objects.

Writing for the *Journal of Experimental Psychology*, Dale N. Swanton et al. introduce their paper in formal academic language complete with scholarly references:

Averaging of Temporal Memories by Rats by Dale N. Swanton, Cynthia M. Gooch, and Matthew S. Matell

> The ability of organisms to behave in accordance with the temporal relationships between events in the world is important for survival (Bateson, 2003; Brunner, Kacelnik, & Gibbon, 1992), and has recently been proposed to play a central role in associative learning (Gallistel & Gibbon, 2000; Kirkpatrick & Church, 2000; Miller & Barnet, 1993). Timing in the seconds to minutes range, interval timing, has been demonstrated in a wide range of species, ranging from honeybees to humans (Boisvert & Sherry, 2006; Henderson, Hurly, Bateson, & Healy, 2006; Rakitin et al., 1998), and shows characteristic features such as flexibility (i.e., animals are able to time stimuli that have randomly occurring onsets) and relativity (i.e., the magnitude of errors is directly proportional to the interval being timed).

Rewriting this for a group of grade four students sounds like this:

Rats can tell time. It helps them learn and survive.

Vocabulary, level of formality, precision of evidence, and documentation of sources vary as you write for different audiences.

Compare the following two articles and the authors' comments on their own writing. The first article is written for a diverse audience; the second article is aimed at academics.

Dinosaur Farts May Have Warmed Ancient Earth by Jennifer Welsh

> We might want to rename the Brachiosaurus with the moniker Gassiosaurus, new research indicates. The gassy emissions from these giant dinosaurs may have been enough to warm the Earth, the researchers say.

Sauropods are large plant-eating dinosaurs typified by such titans as Apatosaurus (once known as Brontosaurus) and Brachiosaurus. When they lived, during the Mesozoic era — from about 250 million years ago until the dinosaurs died out 65 million years ago — the climate was warm and wet. Nothing on Earth today compares with these giants.

Source: liveScience.com — "LiveScience brings readers into the world of science, health and technology."

Audience: Science Curious and Science Buffs, Adults 18-54

Jennifer Welsh: Audience

Jennifer Welsh is Science Editor at *Business Insider*. She has written for *Wired Science, The Scientist, Discover Magazine*, and *LiveScience. com* among others.

In writing this story [*Dinosaur Farts May Have Warmed Ancient Earth*] I had to think about my audience and what they do and don't know. At LiveScience our content is posted throughout the internet on many big sites like msnbc.com and Yahoo!NEWS, so we reach a large audience — most of whom probably don't know anything about methane, what a sauropod is, or when the Mesozoic was. Those all needed to be simplified, especially in the title. Plus, farts are just funny. And dinosaur farts? Comedic gold.

Could Methane Produced By Sauropod Dinosaurs Have Helped Drive Mesozoic Climate Warmth? by David M. Wilkinson, Euan G. Nisbet, and Graeme D. Ruxton

Mesozoic sauropods, like many modern herbivores, are likely to have hosted microbial methanogenic symbionts for the fermentative digestion of their plant food [1]. Today methane from livestock is a significant component of the global methane budget [2]. Sauropod methane emission would probably also have been considerable. Here, we use a simple quantitative approach to estimate the magnitude of such methane production and show that the production of the 'greenhouse' gas methane by sauropods could have been an important factor in warm Mesozoic climates. Sauropod dinosaurs include the largest terrestrial animals known and exhibit a distinctive body shape, featuring a small head at the end of a very long neck.

Source: *Current Biology* — "Current Biology is a general journal that publishes original research across all areas of biology...."

Audience: Research Scientists, Technicians, Lab Directors

David M. Wilkinson: Accessibility

Dr. David M. Wilkinson is the award winning author of *Fundamental Processes in Ecology: An Earth Systems Approach* and co-author (Tom Sherratt) of *Big Questions in Ecology and Evolution*.

Current Biology is a leading journal for the publication of research papers in biology; in addition, it has a magazine section with more general articles aimed at biologists. All the research papers it publishes are relatively short and the section of the journal to which we were submitting our calculations on the potential role of herbivorous dinosaurs on atmospheric chemistry has an especially tight word limit (a maximum of only 1000 words).

To explain any new research result in such a short article requires a very tight prose style – without any wasted words. Although we were writing to be read by research scientists these would not necessarily be experts on dinosaurs – for example scientists with an interest in climate and/or atmospheric chemistry were also likely to be interested in this work. Therefore we added some comments which were designed to make the article more accessible to them, for example explaining that the sauropod dinosaur Apatosaurus louise is also colloquially known as Brontosaurus (this would be unnecessary if writing for an audience of just dinosaur specialists).

The only place in the manuscript where we managed to get away with a somewhat more literary prose style was in the acknowledgements where we wrote, "We thank the late Lynn Margulis for infecting us with her microbial enthusiasm — she would have savoured the notion of sauropods as walking methanogen vats." In a formal research paper the acknowledgments usually receive less editorial scrutiny and so this is often the place where you can get away with a less informal prose style – sometimes even a (supposedly) humorous comment or bad pun!

Consider the nature of your audience: gender, age range, average education, occupations, and expectations. Guest speakers always inquire about the nature of their audience. Bloggers read dozens of posts before commenting. Students become familiar with the interests and language of academic disciplines by reading textbooks and attending lectures. If you are writing for a grade in an educational setting, the best audience research strategy is this: Take your keyword, genre, and goal to your instructor and ask, "Am I on the right track?"

Chapter Three Summary - Consider Your Audience

Shape your message by understanding your audience.

Subject: Canadian Identity

Keyword: Cold

Working Title: Cold: What Is A Canadian?

Genre: Definition

Link: This essay <u>defines</u> what a Canadian is by *describing* three choices that Canadians make: our choice of sports arenas, our choice of real estate, and our choice of pastimes.

Audience: My geography professor, Dr. Brust, is a founding member and director of the Ridge Valley Curling Club. Dr. Brust plays recreational hockey on weekends and has a daughter in figure skating. Dr. Brust is open minded and welcomes all points of view provided they are logical and well-documented.

Add audience to your keyword goal and genre board. As you write, keep asking yourself this question: How will my readers react to this sentence?

Knowing How
To Say It

As You Write

As you write, you create an introduction, middle paragraphs, and a conclusion. Each section of your composition plays a distinct role.

The Introduction

Your introduction establishes the context of your writing. Context includes your reason for writing, your main idea, and your key points. An introduction is like an academic abstract or an executive summary in that it stands on its own. It succinctly communicates the specific purpose and direction of your writing. But it is more than a point of entry or an outline; it creates a common ground for author and audience.

The Middle Paragraphs

Middle paragraphs explore and support the key points outlined in your introduction. This is where you provide the reader with a guided tour of your keyword and key idea from your unique viewpoint. This is where you observe, explain, and document the world as you see it.

The Conclusion

By returning to the themes established in your introduction, your conclusion brings your essay full circle and creates a logical ending. This involves more than a simple summary. It also requires explaining the importance of the journey.

As you write, think of yourself as a tour guide: Start with an orientation session that sets the context for the journey. In the middle of the journey highlight and comment on points of interest. When you return home, acknowledge all that you have seen and the significance of your observations.

FOUR
The Introduction

Establish A Shared Context

We don't see things as they are; we see them as we are.

– Anaïs Nin

Having identified your keyword, key idea, and audience, writing begins. And it begins by writing your introduction.

We all see the world through a slightly different lens because of our individual experiences and expectations. Writing is successful when readers see the world through your lens. So, your introduction must create a common ground for author and audience, a mutual set of meanings and expectations.

This shared context is the foundation for communicating your point of view. It makes your introduction the most important part of your composition.

Create a shared context by identifying your keyword, genre, and goal and by declaring and explaining the link between them. As you compose your introduction, be obvious and specific:

> A. Start With A Descriptive Title
>
> B. Consider An Epigraph
>
> C. Set The Stage
>
> D. Outline Your Key Idea

Sometimes, writers feel that if they are too obvious, all subtlety is lost and their writing appears unimaginative and heavy-handed. They feel like withholding their best idea and building towards a powerful or surprise conclusion.

Resist the temptation. State your goal with precision and detail, make your genre obvious, and outline your main idea in your introduction:

Is The Answer Blowing in the Wind by J.G. Slootweg and W.L. Kling

Wind power is the most rapidly growing technology for renewable power generation. However, fundamental differences exist between conventional thermal, hydro, and nuclear generation and wind power. These differences are reflected in the specific interaction of wind turbines with the power system. Further, there are differences between the various wind turbine types, which also affect their system interaction. In this article, first the current status and the technology of wind power are briefly discussed. The general working principles are explained and the different wind turbine types are described. Then, the differences between wind power and conventional power generation are highlighted as well as their consequences for interaction with the power system, both locally and on a system level.

The amount of time spent developing context depends on the scope and scale of your writing. In *Teaching for Diversity and Social Justice* the authors set aside an entire chapter: "This chapter sets in context the approach to oppression and social justice described in this book."

The length of your introduction is relative to the overall length of your composition. A 50,000 word book calls for a chapter. In a 2000 word essay, a 500 word memo, or a 20 minute speech, a paragraph is often enough. The important thing is that you set the stage before the curtain goes up.

A. Start With A Descriptive Title

Write a descriptive title that stakes out your territory. Include your keyword in the title.

Titles such as *Believers, Moves,* and *Wrong, Wrong, Wrong* are ineffective because they offer no insight regarding the author's subject or intention. However, the following titles work because each author's subject is crystal clear. The titles are like road signs announcing a destination:

> *9 Essential Tips Every Investor Should Know* by Bridget McCrea
>
> *Are Bank Stocks Safe?* by Joe Light
>
> *Rating Retirement Advice: A Critical Assessment of Retirement Planning Software* by John Turner

Here are four strategies for composing titles that provide a clear sense of direction.

1. Combine Your Keyword With An Informative, Specific Subtitle

Your keyword, as discussed in Chapter One, often makes a perfect title, but include an explanatory subtitle indicating your route:

> *Thirst: Water and Power in the Ancient World* by Steven Mithen

Quiet: The Power of Introverts in a World That Can't Stop Talking by Susan Cain

Titan: The Life of John D. Rockefeller, Sr. by Ron Chernow

Nudge: Improving Decisions About Health, Wealth, and Happiness by Richard H. Thaler and Cass R. Sunstein

Drift: The Unmooring of American Military Power by Rachel Maddow

2. Combine A Main Title With A Descriptive, Detailed Subtitle

The following titles unmistakably reveal the authors' intentions:

Waking the Giant: How A Changing Climate Triggers Earthquakes, Tsunamis And Volcanoes by Bill McGuire

Why Nations Fail: The Origins of Power, Prosperity, and Poverty by Daron Acemoglu and James Robinson

Going Solo: The Extraordinary Rise and Surprising Appeal of Living Alone by Eric Klinenberg

Reinventing Fire: Bold Business Solutions for the New Energy Era by Amory Lovins

A provocative title also works as long as the subtitle tells readers what road they are travelling:

Why Can't You Read My Mind? Overcoming the 9 Toxic Thought Patterns that Get in the Way of a Loving Relationship by Jeffrey Bernstein and Susan Magee

To Heaven and Back: A Doctor's Extraordinary Account of Her Death, Heaven, Angels, and Life Again: A True Story by Mary C. Neal

You Are Not So Smart: Why You Have Too Many Friends on Facebook, Why Your Memory Is Mostly Fiction, and 46 Other Ways You're Deluding Yourself by David McRaney.

Why Is It Always About You? The Seven Deadly Sins of Narcissism by Sandy Hotchkiss and James F. Masterson

"*What Color Is The Parachute You Used To Move Your Cheese While Winning Friends And Influencing People In India?* With a title like that, my book can't miss!"

3. Ask A Question

Titles that ask a question stake out your territory in a concise, immediate, and unambiguous manner:

> *Who Killed Alexander the Great?* by James Romm
>
> *Why Do People Smoke?* by Brenda Shoss
>
> *Why Don't Animals Have Wheels?* by Richard Dawkins

4. Include A Number

Numbers in titles are another efficient and accurate way of creating an obvious starting point and specific direction:

> *The Six Secrets of Change: What the Best Leaders Do to Help Their Organizations Survive and Thrive* by Michael Fullan
>
> *The 7 Habits of Highly Effective People: Powerful Lessons in Personal Change* by Stephen R. Covey
>
> *Eight Ways To Save The Planet* by Thomas Kostigen

Ask yourself this: Can readers tell from my title what I am writing about and where I am headed?

B. Consider An Epigraph

An epigraph is a quotation appearing after the title and before the opening paragraph. It indicates the theme of your writing.

> *Debt: Why You Can't Afford To Retire Early*
> *Neither a borrower nor a lender be* —Shakespeare

Starting with a quotation not only suggests your thesis, it also creates an excellent first impression: you appear well-read, educated, and cultured. In addition, when quoting a respected and renowned author, you borrow the authority of the person quoted. Not a bad start.

In *Chicken Soup for the Sister's Soul: Inspirational Stories About Sisters and Their Changing Relationships*, each of the book's 101 stories begins with an epigraph. Some quotations are from famous people; some are from less famous people. The authors also use anonymous quotations.

The reason all the epigraphs work in *Chicken Soup* is that every quotation is relevant; each is in perfect harmony with the story it precedes.

C. Set The Stage

Prepare readers for your key idea by explaining the motivation and the backdrop for your writing. This establishes a common ground for you and your audience and lends an air of inevitability to your main idea.

For example, Parry sets the stage for writing about mosquitoes by immediately establishing the scope and urgency of a global problem:

Re-Engineering Mosquitoes To Fight Disease by Hadyn Parry

> So I'd like to start by focusing on the world's most dangerous animal.
>
> Now, when you talk about dangerous animals, most people might think of lions or tigers or sharks. But of

course the most dangerous animal is the mosquito. The mosquito has killed more humans than any other creature in human history. . . . And the mosquito has killed more humans than wars and plague.

Lee similarly establishes the context for his writing:

Enbridge Pipe Dreams And Nightmares: The Economic Costs And Benefits Of The Proposed Northern Gateway Pipeline by Marc Lee

> The proposed Enbridge northern gateway pipeline (NGP) is a $5 billion investment that, if approved, will transport 525,000 barrels per day of Alberta's oil sands bitumen to Kitimat, BC, where it would be shipped by super-tanker to China. Supporters of the NGP argue that it is in Canada's national economic interest to diversify oil and gas trade to Asia, and that the pipeline will promote economic growth. Enbridge gives the impression of substantial new jobs from the NGP, and claims that the pipeline will create 63,000 person-years of employment during its construction phase, and 1,146 full-time jobs once completed.

Here are seven methods for creating a shared context and preparing readers for your key idea.

Ask A Question

When you start with a question, readers immediately know what prompted your writing and what your subject is:

Google's New Wind Power Deal Shows Real Corporate Leadership by David Pomerantz

> When's the last time you felt really good about something a corporation has done for the environment?
>
> If you're like me, it's probably not recently. Big companies usually grace Greenpeace's blog for destroying the environment.

Today though, we can feel good about at least one company's actions: Google announced that it is purchasing 48 megawatts of clean, renewable wind power for its data centre in Oklahoma, USA. That's enough clean energy to power a small city!

History in Schools and the Problem of "The Nation" by Terry Haydn

This paper considers two questions related to the teaching of history in schools. First, to what extent should school history be based around the teaching of the story of the nation's past? And second, to what extent should the teaching of the national past attempt to present a positive picture of the nation's past, rather than a dispassionately objective and critical one?

The Pursuit of Happiness by Clifton B. Parker

Is happiness everything it's cracked up to be?

It depends. Throughout the ages, our greatest thinkers found happiness an inherently slippery thing to measure or define. Ancient Greek philosophers racked their brains in search of the cleverest answer to this question, and the brightest Enlightenment sages deeply pondered one of humanity's most perplexing and popular subjects.

Times change, and today we live in a huge-bandwidth world with learning and growing opportunities unimagined by our ancestors. Still, these two existential questions remain for us as they did for Aristotle: What is happiness, and how do we achieve it?

Questions are an efficient way of building context and focusing the reader's attention:

The Cost of the Savings and Loan Crisis: Truth and Consequences by Timothy Curry and Lynn Shibut

It has been more than a decade since enactment of the Financial Institutions Reform, Recovery, and Enforcement Act of 1989 (FIRREA), which began the taxpayers' involvement in the cleanup of the savings and loan industry.[1] Over time, misinformation about the cost of the crisis has been widespread; some published reports have placed the cost at less than $100 billion, and others as high as $500 billion.[2] Now that the cleanup is nearly complete, we can answer the following questions about a debacle that has consumed the nation for years:

- What was the total cost of the crisis?

- How much of the total was borne by the U.S. taxpayer?

- How much was borne by the thrift industry?

- How do the actual costs compare with those predicted before and during the cleanup years?

Present A Definition

Presenting a definition of your keyword in your introduction is an ideal method for establishing a shared context. The classic technique involves citing a dictionary definition and then focusing on those elements of the definition that connect to your key idea:

Bullying: The Toxic Workplace

> The Oxford English Dictionary defines bullying as "overbearing insolence; personal intimidation; petty tyranny." When these three forms of bullying occur in the workplace, they create a poisoned environment known as the toxic workplace. This report looks at how workplace bullying harms employees in terms of physical, mental, and emotional health.

Explaining the origin of a word is another common way of leading the reader to your main idea:

The Mortgage: Till Death Do Us Part

> The word mortgage has its origins in the French words *mort*, as in death, and *gage*, as in pledge. Add to that the Latin root *mortuum vadium*, and the word literally means dead pledge. In spite of the fact that a mortgage seems eternal, the pledge dies in one of two ways: either the debt is repaid and the obligation is dead, or the borrower defaults and the deal is dead. This article discusses killing the obligation.

Depending on the conventions of your genre and the audience's expectations, a more sophisticated definition may be needed. Writing for an academic audience accustomed to formal documentation, the authors of the following article carefully define and document their keyword:

Childhood Bullying: A Review of Constructs, Concepts, and Nursing Implications by Jianghong Liu and Nicola Graves

> Bullying among school-age children continues to gain more recognition as an important problem. In the United States, prevalence rates of bullying or having been bullied at school at least once in the last 2 months have been reported at 20.8% physical, 53.6% verbal, 51.4% social, and 13.6% electronic (Wang, 2009). Bullying is most formally defined and most commonly framed in terms of the psychological deficits and social role of the bully. According to Kim, Boyce, Koh, and Leventhal (2009), bullying is a form of aggressive behavior in which individuals in a dominant position intend to cause mental and/or physical suffering to others, and this behavior leads to significant psychological, physical, and emotional sequelae in bullies, victims, and bully/victims.

> However, three decades of research on bullying has led

to numerous definitions of bullying (Barboza, 2009). For instance, Smorti, Menesini, and Smith (2003) pointed out that the definition of bullying is complex because it is characterized by three factors: (1) the bully's intention to cause harm to the victim, (2) the cause of harm being the perceived imbalance of power between the bully and the victim, and (3) the repetition of bullying behavior over time (Farrington, 1993; Olweus, 1999; Smith & Brain, 2000). Any variation in the three criteria can lead to different definitions of bullying. Further complications are introduced by the fact that different languages use different definitions and terms to describe bullying (Smith et al., 1999). Furthermore, parents' and teachers' awareness of children's victimization obfuscate the conceptualization of bullying (Morita, Soeda, Soeda, & Taki, 1999; Rigby, 1994, 1997; Smith et al., 1999).

Despite the variability in its definition, bullying is generally considered a specific type of aggression in which: (1) the behavior is intended to harm or disturb, (2) the behavior occurs repeatedly over time, and (3) there is an imbalance of power, with a more powerful person or group attacking a less powerful one.

Starting your work with a definition does not mean your genre is definition. It is simply an introductory strategy.

Clifton B. Parker: Writing Introductions

Mr. Parker is the Senior Publications Editor and Associate Editor of *UC Davis Magazine* for the University of California.

Introductions serve as the foundation for what content is to follow, and in this sense, are arguably the most significant element of a written body of work. They work best when they are short and sweet, concise and clear, and always reflective of the reader's attention. By the latter I mean that introductions must excite, compel and tantalize the reader to continue on through the rest of the article. Easily said perhaps, but not always easily done. Rewriting and editing the introduction into a polished gem that shines a path onward is an act of intuitiveness, due diligence and craftsmanship. We must always be respectful of the reader's time and effort — and hook 'em early through the introduction.

Provide A Chronology

Locate your key idea in time. This typically involves providing an overview or survey of the circumstances surrounding your main idea.

The History of Happiness by Clifton B. Parker

> Thinking and philosophizing about happiness date to the dawn of civilization, though ideas about what happiness is and how to achieve it have changed dramatically. Aristotle valued intellectual powers over practical ones. . . . For most ancient Greeks, happiness was largely bound up with notions of luck and fortune. . . . Later, in the Middle Ages, the issue focused on one's relationship to God, but Enlightenment thinkers in the 17th and 18th centuries saw it more as a self-evident truth. . . . Indeed, in 1776, America's Founding Fathers declared the "pursuit of happiness" to be one of man's "unalienable rights," along with life and liberty. In the 19th century, Mattey noted, British utilitarians like John Stuart Mill sought to define and measure the value of actions by how much happiness they produce, the quality of that happiness, and how it was distributed throughout society.

New Music for Canada by John Brotman

> The struggle Canadian contemporary classical music

composers face to have their music performed and heard has been experienced by many of them as a continuing civil war. The enemy has not been so much the indifferent public; rather, the musical establishment of orchestras, opera companies, concert presenters and broadcasters are perceived to have constructed a defensive mainstream moat surrounding their programming. The history of neglect, or rebuff after a single performance, has been a constant obstacle for close to a century. One thinks of Harry Somers' opera, Louis Riel, for example: commissioned by the Canadian Opera Company for the 1967 centennial, and successfully received, it has barely been professionally produced thereafter. The many ensembles dedicated to the commissioning and performance of new music mostly work on a smaller scale, pay small royalties, and are hard-pressed to offer more than a minimal number of performances after the premieres; larger ensembles – orchestras, for example – seem to confine their contemporary commitment to one- or two-a year events.

John Weinzweig and John Beckwith both waged this battle throughout their careers.

Present Statistics And Facts

Evidence and support for your point of view is not restricted to the middle paragraphs of your compositions. Presenting factual data in your introduction provides a solid backdrop for your ideas.

As is the case with everything you write, your information must be relevant and accurate; data must come from reliable sources.

The Plight Of Younger Workers by Francis Fong

Two weeks ago, (March 8, 2012) TD Economics

released a brief report (*Older Workers Stampede into the Labour Market*) highlighting the surge in job creation among Canadians over 60 years of age during the recession and subsequent recovery. In this report, we chronicle the fortunes of those at the opposite end of the age spectrum (those aged 15-24 years). The story for young workers has been the mirror image of their older counterparts. Of the more than 430,000 net jobs lost over the course of the recession, more than half were concentrated among those under the age of 25 years. This occurred despite the fact that they only accounted for one-in-six (16.5%) in the labour force. Even after the recession's end, the recovery has been almost non-existent for youth in aggregate – just 1,300 net jobs have been added over the last two and a half years. In contrast, employment among those over the age of 25 years is currently a striking 400,000 jobs above its pre-recession level.

As chart 1 reveals, it is the very young that have suffered the worst.

GHA Report 2012 by Development Initiatives

In 2010 major natural disasters in Haiti and Pakistan had wide-ranging effects on the collective humanitarian response: driving up overall international spending by 23% over the previous year. . . .

In 2011 global humanitarian needs were smaller in scale, with the UN's consolidated humanitarian appeal requesting US$8.9 billion, 21% less in financing, to meet the humanitarian needs of 62 million people, compared with US$11.3 billion requested to meet the needs of 74 million people in 2010. The overall international humanitarian financing response fell back by 9%, from

US$18.8 billion in 2010 to US$17.1 billion in 2011. But despite the reduction in needs in the UN's humanitarian appeals, the gap in unmet financing widened to levels not seen in ten years.

Move From The General To The Specific

Moving from the general to the specific is the cinematic equivalent of starting with a wide angle view of a landscape and then gradually drawing closer and closer until the focus is on one object in the scene.

The following introduction uses this general approach. The author starts with a high-level overview and then quickly zooms in and focuses on his key idea: there is a connection between insects and dreams. In the following excerpt, the square brackets refer to footnotes:

The Curious Connection Between Insects and Dreams by Barrett A. Klein

> Insects are diverse, resourceful, and resilient, serving as symbols of everything from beauty [1] and rebirth [2], to pestilence and evil [3]. Insects pollinate or devour crops [4], contribute to [5-7] or wreak havoc on technology [8-10], inspire architecture [11-14] or obliterate it [15,16], and advance human health [4,17-20] or vector disease [21,22]. Insects inhabit nearly every earthly niche but in the deep marine [23], and can be found among, on, and even inside humans [22,24], and thus it is no surprise that insects have also made their way into our dreams.

In the next example, the author starts with a high-level overview then narrows the view by referring to a particular example that exemplifies his key idea:

Context: Controlling What People Expect To See

> Cognitive science tells us that we are all subject to

confirmation bias. That is, we select information that confirms what we already believe. By extension, the corollary is true: we selectively dismiss information that does not support our beliefs. In other words, we see best what we expect to see and miss the rest.

Search YouTube for the phrase *Pearls Before Breakfast* and you will find a video of a handsome young violinist in casual dress busking in the lobby of a metro station. His performance of works by Bach and Schubert is sublime. But of the thousand people who pass by, less than a dozen glance in his direction. He makes about thirty dollars.

Playing an instrument valued at approximately four million dollars, the busker is Joshua Bell. Regarded as one of the world's finest concert violinists. Audiences normally greet him with thunderous applause and bid farewell with a standing ovation.

Why did everyone in the station ignore him? The stage was not set. In fact, there was no stage; no chandeliers; no plush seating. The context was wrong.

In *Fire Door*, Ani Difranco sings, "Taken out of context, I must seem so strange." However, by controlling the context, what seems strange becomes familiar.

Writing about wind power and health issues, Fenster similarly starts with a wide angle view and then focuses on specific issues. It is the written equivalent of watching a camera lens zoom in closer and closer as it moves from Canada, to Ontario, to people living near wind turbines, to a blood pressure cuff:

Are Wind Farms Really Bad for People's Health? by Ariel Fenster

At present wind turbines produce a little over 2% of Canada's electricity. The industry's goal is to have this number go up to 20% by 2025 leading to a rapid expansion of wind farms around the country. In Ontario, wind power for the first time has surpassed coal in the production of electricity. This is good news in terms of greenhouse gas emission but it may come at a cost. More and more people living nearby, blame wind turbines for a variety of health problems. The symptoms vary but include sleep deprivation, anxiety, depression, and increased blood pressure.

Move From The Specific To The General

Moving from a single example to a broader observation often involves relating a story. Starting with a real-world example humanizes a topic and makes it more accessible and immediate for your audience:

How To Remember Things by Alex Lickerman

> I once came up with a metaphor I thought perfectly captured the sheer mass of material my classmates and I were expected to memorize in our first two years of medical school: it was like being asked to enter a grocery store and memorize the names of every product in the store, their number and location, every ingredient in every product in the order in which they appear on the food label, and then to do the same thing in every grocery store in the city. When I look back now I can't imagine how any of us were able to do it. And yet we did.

Scarf similarly shares a personal moment while setting the stage for a discussion of happiness:

The Happiness Syndrome by Maggie Scarf

> "Happiness cannot be pursued; it must ensue," I once counseled my then-adolescent daughter, Susie. I was quoting the psychoanalyst-philosopher Victor Frankl. Susie countered that she couldn't "buy into" this point of view; it was buying into passivity. I rejoined with a

quote from Hawthorne, which was, as I recollected: "Happiness is like a butterfly, which, if you chase after it, will elude you. If, however, you sit quietly and wait, it will come and light upon your shoulder." Susie suggested a butterfly net -- an argument that had a certain undeniable merit.

Your Rebel Brain by Jeff Wise

Idaho hunter Nolan Koller was sitting near a maple tree, hoping for an elk to appear, when his walkie-talkie crackled to life. "Dad," said his son Jason. "There's a bear cub."

You can refine and develop the ways you respond to fear, which could one day save your life. Some advice for keeping your rebel brain under control. . . .

Sam McNerney: Writing Introductions

Mr. McNerney's writing has appeared on *ScientificAmerican.com*, *BBC Focus*, and *Huffingtonpost.com*. He maintains the column *The Cognitive Philosopher* at *CreativityPost.com*, and blogs at *Moments of Genius* on *BigThink.com*.

My primary goal in the opening paragraph is for the reader to crave the second paragraph. Writers use the metaphor of a hook to describe the role of an opening paragraph; it should lure the reader into the second paragraph. I agree, but the hook shouldn't be obvious. The attraction of an opening paragraph should almost hypnotize a reader; it should make him forget he is reading. There are many ways to accomplish this.

Make An Interesting Observation

An interesting observation reveals an unexpected fact or identifies a way of looking at a situation that is contrary to popular thought:

A green, raw, hot chili pepper contains five times more vitamin C than an orange.

If you flipped a coin 99 times and it came up heads every time, the chances of it coming up tails on the 100th consecutive toss are exactly the same as the first time it was tossed.

There are no nuts and no grapes in Post Grape-Nuts® breakfast cereal.

However, keep in mind that what is uncommon knowledge for one audience might be common sense for another. An astronaut would not be surprised by the following facts, but many others might be:

Why Are Astronauts Weightless in Space? by Nancy Atkinson

When asked why objects and astronauts in spacecraft appear weightless, many people give these answers:

1. There is no gravity in space and they do not weigh anything.
2. Space is a vacuum and there is no gravity in a vacuum.
3. The astronauts are too far away from Earth's surface to be subject to its gravitational pull.

These answers are all wrong!

D. Outline Your Key Idea

The last part of your introduction outlines your key idea. Your key idea is your contract with the reader. And, like any good contract, it creates a shared understanding by setting expectations, providing detail, and avoiding surprises.

This process began in Chapter Two by linking your goal and genre. In the following examples, the goal is italicized and the genre is underlined:

This article *explains* why winter tires are safer on ice than all season tires <u>by comparing</u> them.

This essay *describes* three types of neurons <u>by classifying</u> them according to function.

This blog *teaches* you how to post a tweet <u>by providing a step by step set of instructions</u>.

Complete your introduction by taking the link you developed in Chapter Two and adding details. Your goal and genre become clearer as you provide more information. Often, all it takes is a few significant details:

This article *explains* why winter tires are safer on ice than all season tires <u>by comparing</u> traction, control, and stopping distances.

This essay *describes* three types of neurons <u>by classifying</u> them according to function: sensory, integrative, and motor.

This blog *teaches* you how to post a tweet <u>by providing a step by step set of instructions</u> complete with annotated screen captures and FAQs.

Instead of writing, "This article discusses stress," be specific and obvious:

This article investigates three causes of work-related stress: incompetent management, unsafe working conditions, and toxic social environments.

Instead of writing, "This blog *helps* insomniacs," provide detail:

This blog helps you sleep better by identifying four causes of insomnia: stress, anxiety, medication, and diet (Mayo Clinic).

Note how the writing improves as the level of detail increases:

This report compares solar and wind power.

This report proves that wind power is better than solar power by comparing them.

This report *argues* that wind power is more cost effective than solar power <u>by comparing</u> three factors: start-up costs, maintenance, scalability.

State your goal. Describe your approach. Include the details of your approach (italics added):

Reasons Why We Forget by Kendra Cherry

What are some of the major reasons why we forget information? One of today's best known memory researchers, Elizabeth Loftus, has identified four major reasons why people forget: *retrieval failure, interference, failure to store, and motivated forgetting.*

9 Reasons Golf Is Good For Your Brain by Erin Matlock

Golf is a game that not only challenges your physical skill but also your ability to stay calm and focused. It turns out, it's also a great way to boost your brain power. No matter what your handicap, *golf can provide a fun, social way to stimulate your brain, increase your self esteem, and sharpen your concentration.* Here's how.

The Pursuit of Happiness by Clifton B. Parker

There is progress to report. Faculty members at UC Davis are leaders in the study of the "science of happiness." And while happiness research is in its infancy, three major points are emerging:

- *the positive trumps the negative*
- *social participation trumps materialism*
- *generosity trumps selfishness*

Because readers see best what they expect to see and tend to block out the rest, your success as a writer, communicating your point of view and connecting with your audience, depends on creating a shared context, a shared set of expectations. Context is the gravity that grounds writing. Sharing your ideas starts with sharing your context and setting expectations.

For example, when psychologists had people watch a video and count how many times a ball was passed among a group of basketball players, 46% of the audience did not notice when a person in a gorilla suit strolled through the scene, faced the camera, and pounded his chest.

In a similar experiment, 75% of the people walking through the central plaza of Western Washington University did not see a clown ride his unicycle around a large sculpture in the plaza on a bright sunny afternoon. He was dressed in a purple jumpsuit, polka dot shirt, red and yellow clown shoes, and sported a big red nose.

However, not a single person would have missed them if the researchers had said, "Watch for a gorilla, or watch for a clown." For details of the experiments see The Invisible Gorilla by Christopher Chabris and Daniel Simons and Did You See the Unicycling Clown? by Ira E. Hyman Jr. et al.

As you write your introduction, be specific; be obvious; be detailed. Manage and direct your readers' expectations.

The Canadian And American Health Care Systems by Odette Madore

> This paper presents a comparative description of the Canadian and American health care systems and reviews the most recent literature. The first part briefly examines the reasons for and against government involvement in health care; the second part compares both systems in terms of access, financial barriers to care, extent of benefits, and administration; the third section deals with cost containment. Finally comparisons are made in terms of the quality of care.

Firearms and Violent Crime by Mia Dauvergne and Leonardo De Socio

Using data from Statistics Canada's Uniform Crime Reporting (UCR) and Homicide Surveys, this Juristat examines the prevalence of firearm-related violent crime in Canada at the national, provincial/territorial and census metropolitan area levels. It presents the incidence and trends in overall firearm violence and the characteristics of those offences most often committed with a firearm. It also compares the incidence of firearm-related homicide in Canada to that in other countries. Finally, data from the Integrated Criminal Courts Survey is used to compare court processing and sentencing outcomes between firearm and non-firearm violent offences.

Comparing Democratic Maturity Test Scores For German And American College Freshman by Rosemarie Kolstad, et al.

The study sought to compare scores on The Democratic Maturity Test between German and American college freshman students. The test is designed to measure two things: (1) personal maturity, and (2) social integration. The American students were significantly superior in personal maturity, and the German students were significantly superior in social integration.

Obama vs. Romney: A Stark Contrast on the Environment by Fen Montaigne

Few policy issues separate Barack Obama and Mitt Romney more widely than the environment and energy. One man believes human activity is driving global warming, the other questions to what extent humans are responsible. One advocates federal support for renewable energy technologies, the other believes that alternative energy should sink or swim on its own merits. One believes that the U.S. government can play an important role in setting standards that are environmentally and financially beneficial, the other calls the Environmental Protection Agency "a tool in the hands of the president to crush the private enterprise system."

What follows is a summary of the positions of the two candidates on four key issues:

- Climate Change

- Oil and Gas Drilling

- Renewable Energy and Energy Efficiency

- The EPA and Environmental Regulation

In the following examples, the authors meticulously outline their areas of interest, their goal, the limits of their research, and their four main questions, and then foreshadow their conclusion:

The Case For And Against Onshore Wind Energy In The UK by Samuela Bassi, Alex Bowen and Sam Fankhauser

> The aim of this policy brief is to inform the debate about the role of onshore wind energy in meeting the UK's future electricity needs and achieving its environmental objectives. The brief does not provide new empirical estimates – there are many such numbers already published. We contribute to the debate by identifying the most credible estimates available and drawing some key policy lessons from that information. Some robust conclusions can indeed be drawn, but this does not mean the evidence base is perfect. Data on energy technologies and their future development are subject to uncertainty and may change over time, so we recommend that this issue continues to be monitored and investigated in future research.

> The brief is structured around four key questions:

> How much might onshore wind contribute to the UK

energy mix over the next few decades?

What is the impact of intermittent wind power generation at a large scale on the stability and reliability of the UK's electric power system?

What is the economic cost of onshore wind and how does it compare with other forms of low-carbon energy?

What are the environmental side-effects of onshore wind on the UK's landscapes and ecosystems?

We conclude by suggesting how the acceptability of onshore wind may be enhanced through changes in the policy environment.

Ravelli takes a similarly methodical approach when writing about Canadian and American value differences. His introduction moves from the general to the specific, so he begins by outlining one of the main interests of sociology:

One of sociology's defining interests is the study of the relationship between the individual and society (Brym with Fox, 1989).

He then focuses on a single component:

A critical component of this investigation is the attempt to understand the role culture plays in defining people's perception of their social environment.

Next is a description of how the article will proceed:

The first section of this article reviews the defining characteristics of culture and many of the concepts that sociologists use to analyze and study it. The second section investigates Canadian and American cultural values to determine whether they are different.

The introduction ends with an explanation of his goals:

The purpose of this article then is twofold: the first is to acquaint you with the sociological analyses of culture, and the second is to compare and contrast Canadian and American cultures in the hopes of helping you appreciate what it means to be a Canadian.

Depending on audience expectations and the conventions of the genre, writers sometimes precede their introductions with formal mechanisms such as the abstract, executive summary, bulleted highlights, or a preface. All of these devices serve the same function as an introduction: they create a common ground for author and audience and a shared set of meanings and expectations.

Chapter Four Summary - Establish A Shared Context

Start with a descriptive title. Consider an epigraph. Set the stage. Outline your key idea.

Cold: What Is A Canadian?

I don't trust any country that looks around a continent and says, "Hey, I'll take the frozen part." – Jon Stewart

What word best defines a Canadian? Polite? Bump into a Canadian, spill his coffee, and he will apologize to you. Tolerant? We listen to politicians in both official languages. Inventive? Poutine: a mixture of fries, gravy, and cheese curds. Cold? Voila! Canadians are cold. Not in an emotional sense, but physically. We are freezing; and we love it. We embrace the cold; we shun warmth; we crave the chill. Cold is the Canadian identity. Three examples of 100% Canadian choices prove my point: our choice of sports arenas, our choice of real estate, and our choice of pastimes.

As you write your introduction, ask yourself this: Have I explained the context for my writing and directed my readers' expectations?

FIVE
The Middle

Conduct A Guided Tour

Professor: Tell me everything you know about frogs.
Student: Frogs eat flies. Now, flies are insects of the order Diptera
from the Greek di meaning two and ptera meaning wings. . . .

When you write, you invite readers on a journey through your mental landscape. From your point of view, it is a well travelled road. All your logic and all your pathways are automatically connected in your mind because they come from your mind. However, nothing is automatic for your readers. They travel in unfamiliar territory.

So, as you write middle paragraphs, think of yourself as a tour guide: take your fellow travellers by the hand and carefully guide them through your terrain. Your introduction was the orientation session describing your destination and your means of travel. The middle of your composition is the tour itself complete with commentary, explanations, navigational aids, and stops at points of interest.

Your middle paragraphs explore, develop, and support your keyword and your key idea. They are organized by following the conventions of your genre and the main points listed in your introduction, and their content depends, in part, on what sort of evidence and documentation your audience expects.

Keep your middle paragraphs short, less than 200 words, for the simple reason that long blocks of text intimidate and discourage readers. We live in a world of the 140 character tweet, the sound bite, instant messaging, and fast food. Each time you move to a new thought or a variation on a thought, create a new paragraph. Do not make one paragraph carry too much weight. Divide ideas into manageable units of thought.

As you write middle paragraphs, think in terms of your contract with the reader, your transitions, the nature of your evidence, and documenting your sources.

1. Keep Your Promise

2. Use Transitional Devices

3. Provide Evidence

4. Document Your Sources

1. Keep Your Promise

Writing is an act of discovery. Nothing clarifies and sharpens your thinking as thoroughly as writing does. As a result, new ideas and different perspectives materialize as you write. However, always keep your introduction and middle paragraphs in harmony.

Your middle paragraphs fulfil the contract established in your introduction. If your key idea promised a description of three items, describe them in the order they were introduced. If, as you write and research, you discover a fourth item or find yourself debating rather than describing, either return to your original promise or revise your introduction.

Google's Two Best Kept Secrets

Google™ is the preeminent search engine on the internet. According to statowl.com, it has 80% of the market share. By comparison, its closest competitor has 9%. Google is so popular that its name is also a verb. According to Google, they process more than 100 billion searches a month. However, for all its popularity, it has two well-kept secrets. This article reveals those secrets and describes the power of *scholar.google* and *images.google*.

Google's ~~Two~~ Three Best Kept Secrets (revision)

Google™ is the preeminent search engine on the internet. According to statowl.com, it has 80% of the market share. By comparison, its closest competitor has 9%. Google is so popular that its name is also a verb. According to Google, they process more than 100 billion searches a month. However, for all its popularity, it has ~~two~~ three well-kept secrets. This article ~~reveals those secrets and~~ describes the power of *site:, scholar.google,* and *images.google* and explains how they work.

2. Use Transitional Devices

Without transitions, ideas appear disjointed, disorganized, and incoherent. That is why we often steer conversations using transitional devices:

Speaking of travel, how much does it cost. . . .

> While we are on the topic of families, I. . . .
>
> I'm going to change the subject for a minute and ask everyone. . . .

With proper transitions, readers can follow you anywhere. A joke popular with graduate students neatly demonstrates this point:

> Each year, PhD candidates in biology faced the ordeal of passing an oral exam before they could graduate. Each year, the examiners demanded comprehensive information about one of two species: "Tell us everything you know about frogs." Or, "Tell us everything you know about flies." A student was assured by classmates that this year's question would be, "Tell us everything you know about flies." So, the student memorized the standard textbooks on flies. Alas, the question was, "Tell us everything you know about frogs." The quick thinking student replied, "Frogs eat flies. Now, flies are insects of the order Diptera from the Greek di meaning two and ptera meaning wings. . . ."

Numbered Transitions

Creating transitions is as simple as using numbers or the words *first*, *second*, and *third*. Basic numbered transitions accurately move the reader from idea to idea and organize and structure your writing.

Tails: Why Humans Need Them

> Imagine being greeted by a dozen people who begin happily wagging their tails the minute they see you. How good would that make you feel? . . . This essay discusses three advantages of humans having tails: 1. Improved Communication, 2. Increased Stability, and 3. Enhanced Agility.
>
> 1. From joyful wagging to submissive tucking, a tail is an unambiguous and valuable communication device.

2. When it comes to stability, nothing beats a tripod.

3. Swinging, climbing, and holding tools are just a few of the examples of the dexterity gained from having a tail.

Wordplay: The Witlessness Protection Program

This blog presents examples of three types of wordplay. First we have puns. Second we have one-liners. Third we have Tom Swifties.

First we have puns. Puns are seen by some as the lowest form of humour; however, others believe that "the pun is mightier than the sword."

Second we have one-liners. The comedian Henny Youngman was known as the "King of the One Liner." He was either very funny or he only owned one ship.

Third we have Tom Swifties. "I have invented dozens of Tom Swifties," Charlie said calculatingly.

In her article, *How To Remember Names – Five Easy Tricks,* Matlock uses the device of numbering her key points:

1) Pay attention.

Obvious, right? You'd be amazed at how little attention we pay to the person we are meeting. Be present in the moment and listen when your new acquaintance says her name. Clear your mind and focus on her – not on what you're going to say next.

2) Repeat the new name. Say it right back to the person.

John: Hi, my name is John. You: John, nice to meet you.

Then, try to use the name two more times before parting. An excellent way to commit a name to memory is to introduce the person to one or two others.

3) Ask for the spelling. . . .

Subheadings

Subheadings work as unerringly as numbered transitions. A restatement of the details listed in your introduction, they make excellent signposts and structure your writing:

Mortgage Insurance Versus Life Insurance

> Home buyers normally buy mortgage insurance. The idea is dead simple: if you die, insurance pays off the mortgage. However, home buyers have a choice of buying the mortgage insurance offered by the lending institution or buying a life insurance policy offered by an insurance agent. The life insurance policy must meet or exceed the amount of the mortgage. Take care. Choosing between the two is not a trivial decision. Consult your lending institution and an insurance expert. It is a steep learning curve, but here are three initial considerations: Cost, Portability, and Value.
>
> Cost
> Compare the cost of the lender's mortgage insurance with the cost of a life insurance policy in the same amount. Also, ask the lending institution if there is a penalty or any administrative charges for not taking their mortgage insurance. Alternatively, are there any incentives for. . . .
>
> Portability
> If you move your mortgage from one institution to another, does the mortgage insurance move with the loan? What happens if. . . .
>
> Value
> Compare the value of the mortgage insurance with the value of the life insurance in twenty years' time. Normally, the value of the mortgage insurance declines as the mortgage declines. However, the value of the life

insurance remains. . . .

Summary
In summary, this is an important financial decision requiring careful research and thought. Talk to experts in the field and. . . .

Puma makes use of subheadings as he lists ten reasons for homeschooling. The repetition creates a sense of unity and provides the framework for his points.

Comparing Homeschooling vs Public Schooling: Ten Reasons for Homeschooling Children by Joe Puma

Reason to Homeschool # 10 – Class size of One

If you ask just about any teacher what the most important factor is in education they will say class size.

Reason to Homeschool # 9 – Arcane Traditions

Do you know why students have the summer off? It is so they can work the fields of their family's farm because 90% of people live in farming communities.

Reason to Homeschool # 8 – Delayed Maturity

By grouping students into similar age groups it slows the maturity of the group as a whole.

Similarly, when Kennan writes about happiness, the subheadings unify and organize his writing and serve as transitional devices:

The Four Levels of Happiness Defined by John Keenan

Level 1
Happiness Derived From Material Objects And The Pleasures They Can Provide.

Level 2
Happiness Derived From Personal Achievement And Ego Gratification.

Level 3
Happiness Derived From Doing Good For Others And
Making The World A Better Place.

Level 4
Ultimate, Perfect Happiness.

Transitional Words And Phrases

The words and phrases used in constructing simple, compound, and complex sentences, as discussed in Chapter Seven, are also valuable connecting devices. The list of words is extensive and familiar: furthermore, however, eventually, as a result, and, but, so. Searching the internet for the phrase *transitional words* uncovers a wealth of word lists and guidelines for creating cohesion and smooth transitions.

Newscasters have mastered the art of using transitions for connecting similar ideas or for abruptly changing direction:

> Experts predict the changes will mean higher taxes for the average Canadian. *In a related story*, mortgage rates are expected to climb.

> Fortunately, both the moose and the cowboy survived. *Now* to sports with Scott Gridiron.

Writers use them in the same way:

> The comedian Henny Youngman is known as the "King of the One Liner." *However*, he started his career as a violinist.

> My wife heard my singing in the shower; *as a result*, singing in the shower is forbidden.

> Dogs are intelligent. *For example*, a border collie named Chaser has a vocabulary of approximately one thousand words.

In the following paragraph, the transitional words and phrases are underlined:

Does Studying Behavioral Economics Improve Your Financial Decisions?
by Sam McNerney

> <u>Here's one more example</u>. Let's say you are on your way
> to the theater with a ticket worth $20 and a $20 bill in
> your wallet. When you arrive at the theater you find
> that you've lost the ticket. The question is: Do you buy
> another ticket with your $20 bill? Most say no. <u>Now</u> take
> the same scenario but instead of having a ticket worth
> $20 and a $20 bill, you have two $20 bills. You arrive at
> the theater, but this time you've lost a $20 bill. Same
> question: Do you buy a ticket? Most say yes. Like the
> previous example, this makes no financial sense because
> twenty dollars is lost in both scenarios. <u>However</u>, for
> some reason people feel that the lost ticket is worth more
> than the lost twenty. <u>Point is</u>, when it comes to money,
> we understand things relatively instead of absolutely.

The phrase "Here's one more example" creates the transition from
paragraph to paragraph. The words "Now" and "However" signal
a change of direction, and the phrase "Point is" indicates a summing
up.

Repeated Words

Repeating exact words, altering the words slightly, or using synonyms
unifies and connects ideas as you move from sentence to sentence or
paragraph to paragraph.

In the following passage, note how the author moves from paragraph
to paragraph by repeating and slightly altering a phrase and using
synonyms. The underlining is mine:

> <u>The question of censorship</u> as it relates to government
> scientists <u>is disturbing</u>.

> <u>The question of censoring</u> government librarians <u>is
> upsetting</u>.

<u>The question of</u> who controls the <u>censors is distressing</u>.

In *Food and Wine Pairing is Just a Big Scam* by Alder Yarrow, the author subtly uses the transitional strategy of repeatedly referring to time as he glides from paragraph to paragraph. The underlining is mine.

> <u>Wine has always</u> gone with food. In fact, one of the first reasons that wine became popular as a beverage was not for its flavor, but because the alcohol helped kill the nasties that often infected pre-refrigerator-technology cuisine. The surest recipe for an unpleasant evening was to forget to drink a bit of wine, usually diluted heavily with water, after gnawing on that side of beef that had been hanging in your medieval "kitchen" for weeks.
>
> <u>It didn't take long</u> for the cultural practice of drinking wine with meals to be cemented as part of civilization, and it's stuck for, oh, the last four thousand years or so. Of course, it didn't hurt that wine also gets us drunk. Don't underestimate the power of fun as a driver of cultural traditions.
>
> <u>Along the way</u> to its peak of popularity, wine started tasting a lot better, especially as winemakers learned more about chemistry, viticulture, and aging wine. At some point, most people started drinking wine more for the pleasure of its flavors than for its digestive benefits, not to mention the fact that, yes, it gets us drunk.
>
> <u>I guess at some point</u>, people started forming opinions that not only was a proper meal incomplete without a bottle of wine, certain wines actually tasted better with certain foods and vice versa.
>
> <u>And that was where</u> everything started to go downhill.

Matlock creates paragraph transitions by repeating words in *9 Reasons Golf Is Good For Your Brain*:

<u>Golf</u> is a <u>game</u> that not only challenges your physical skill but also your ability to stay calm and <u>focused</u>.

When you <u>golf</u>, you not only have to <u>focus</u> on the ball while it's at your feet, but also as it flies over the green.

Many <u>golfers</u> give themselves positive reinforcement during the round.

<u>Golf</u> is often referred to as a <u>game</u> that requires excellent coordination.

In The Happiness Syndrome, Scarf similarly uses repetition for creating cohesion and gliding from idea to idea. She also uses transitional words and the technique of asking a question as navigational aids for the reader. Here are the opening sentences of eight of her paragraphs. The underlining is mine:

<u>At the time</u> of the aforementioned conversation, neither I nor anyone I knew had ever considered whether <u>happiness</u> is a good thing or a bad thing.

<u>Granted</u>, this way of thinking about <u>happiness</u> does seem counterintuitive.

<u>Although</u> what is meant by "<u>happiness</u>" has never been specified, it seems likely, as Bentall observes, that the condition has "affective, cognitive and behavioral components."

What is the frequency of <u>happiness</u>?

What are the causes of <u>happiness</u>?

According to Bentall, one of the most intractable <u>happiness</u>-related problems is its clear-cut association with expansive, celebratory behaviors — eating too much, drinking too much, behaving too impulsively.

<u>Happiness</u> is often related to discernible cognitive abnormalities; happy people regularly exhibit an array

of cognitive distortions and deficits.

While <u>happiness</u> has, he concedes, received little attention from psychopathologists — no formal diagnostic criteria describing the condition are currently available....

Parallel Construction

Parallel construction is an orderly and methodical technique for guiding readers through your ideas. Parallel construction involves formulating a pattern and then using it as a template throughout your composition. In the following example, Percic's template is as follows:

> Provide a Label - Present a Quotation - Write a Description - List Tags

What Kind of Blogger Are You? 7 Different Blogger Types Explained by Eva Percic

> Hedonists: "I blog about life in general and its enjoyments."
>
> Hedonists promote different lifestyles to enrich people's daily routines. They are emotional and are not afraid to express feelings or reach out to others.
>
> Tags: food, travel, sex, shopping, life, entertainment
>
> Techies: "I'm fascinated by new technologies and its applications to various personal and professional fields."
>
> Techies don't get much satisfaction from the writing process, but enjoy spreading their word, sharing knowledge and educating.
>
> Tags: IT, gaming
>
> Professionals: "Blogging is part of my job."
>
> Professionals present accomplishments and seek

feedback from their followers. For them, blogging is all about making connections.

Tags: corporate, consultants, belletristics, copywriters

Parallel construction structures your writing; it makes transitions straightforward; and it leads readers through your landscape in an organized and obvious manner.

If you were writing about types of men, for example, once you create a pattern, the writing flows because you have a template, a master framework. Here is a pattern for describing types of men:

Provide a Label - Name the Vehicles They Drive - Identify the Video They Watch - State What They Read - Describe Their Skills

Stereotypes - Five Types of Men

The Banker

The Banker drives a dependable, fuel efficient, compact car. His PVR records everything on PBS, Oasis HD, and the Discovery Channel. He reads *Maclean's* and *The Globe and Mail*. He does his own taxes and mows his grass in geometrical patterns.

The Athlete

The Athlete rides a bike. He watches ESPN, TSN, the NBA, the NHL, the NFL, and MLB. He has lifetime subscriptions to *Sports Illustrated* and *Runner's World*. He stretches, jogs, works out, pumps iron, and consumes vast quantities of bodybuilding supplements.

The more detailed pattern, the more interesting the writing:

Provide a Label - Name the Vehicles They Do and Do Not Drive - Identify the Video They Will and Will Not Watch - Describe What They Will and Will Not Read - Describe Their Skills and Lack of Skills - Describe Their

Clothes and Aroma

Stereotypes - Five Types of Men

The Scholar

The scholar rides a bicycle or takes a bus; he does not ride in cars unless they are hybrids. He does not watch movies; he watches films. He reads hardcover books and periodicals, not paperbacks and magazines. He can scan a sonnet by Shakespeare, but he cannot shingle a roof. He wears corduroy and plaid and smells like aftershave.

The Redneck

The redneck drives a 4 x 4 truck. Period. He likes movies with plenty of loud full-chested action. He will not watch anything that depends on dialogue. He can read, but he does not read. He can operate a backhoe, skin a moose, and change a ball joint, but he cannot spell. He wears denim and cotton and retains a faint aroma of a tire shop.

3. Provide Evidence

Support your ideas with evidence that is consistent with your goals and appropriate for your audience. One audience may require facts, figures, and footnotes; another audience may be persuaded by a single undocumented example. As you select and present evidence, keep your readers' expectations in mind.

Anecdotes

Anecdotes are true stories. Although they are based on single incidents, writers use them as a platform for supporting generalizations. A true story that humanizes a situation can be as powerful and persuasive as any set of statistics.

Why I Love, Support & Believe in Wind Energy by Meredith Smith MacDonald

My fascination with wind turbines began sometime around 2006. Driving down the 401 eastbound, I noticed the two-blade wind turbine that sat off to my left somewhere around Highgate. I looked at it in wonder and thought to myself, "That is brilliant! Why aren't more farmers generating their own power this way?" A short time later I came across the same style two-blade turbine at a turkey farm just outside of London, once again thinking it was an amazing way to generate power for the turkey barn. Those two-blade turbines planted a seed in my mind that would lie dormant until 2009.

Scarf introduces her essay on happiness with an anecdote concerning her daughter and concludes with an anecdote about her husband:

Introduction

"Happiness cannot be pursued; it must ensue," I once counseled my then-adolescent daughter, Susie. . . . Susie countered that she couldn't "buy into" this point of view; it was buying into passivity.

Conclusion

After everyone had finally departed, my husband's gaze met mine over a river of litter and debris, and I opened my mouth. I was going to say something like, "I wish I were dead," or "Can't we move to Alaska?" when he intervened and said, "Wasn't that the best party, ever? Everyone had a wonderful time."

Statistics depend on empirical proof; anecdotal evidence rests on human truth.

Examples

Examples do more than support your statements. They illustrate, expand, and clarify your ideas. They bring ideas to life and communicate intellectual concepts in an accessible and concrete manner.

Does Studying Behavioral Economics Improve Your Financial Decisions? by Sam McNerney

> [W]e think about money relatively, not absolutely.
>
> <u>For example</u>, let's say you are buying a stereo for $400 when someone tells you that across town is the same stereo for $300. . . . If you're like most people, you'll drive across town and save the 100 bucks. Now, suppose you are buying a car for $30,000 when someone tells you that across town is the same car for $29,900. If you're like most people, you'll forgo the $100 discount and buy the car at $30,000. But given that each scenario is financially identical – a trip across town saves $100 – shouldn't you respond the same? If you were rational, yes. But you aren't; for some reason you feel that the $100 saved in the car scenario is less that the $100 saved in the stereo scenario.
>
> <u>Here's one more example</u>. Let's say you are on your way to the theater with a ticket worth $20 and a $20 bill in your wallet. . . .

What Is Forgiveness? by Hollye Dexter

> Say you're standing in line at the post office and someone accidentally steps on your toe. They quickly move back and say "Sorry!" and you say "No problem." It's over and quickly forgotten. But what if they say "Sorry!" and then continue to stand on your toe? Are you still going to say, "No problem?"

Would Higher Tuition Fees Restrict Access To University Studies? by Norma Kozhaya and Germain Belzile

> On the whole, despite some variations based on the

chosen discipline, the average income of university graduates is much higher than that of people without degrees. For example, a recent study from the Quebec Department of Education[7] found that a high school graduate can expect to earn a lifetime pre-tax income of $1,288,438, compared to $2,166,948 for someone who holds a bachelor's degree.

Statistics

Data is persuasive. Statistics and facts provide compelling support for your statements:

Firearms and Violent Crime by Mia Dauvergne and Leonardo De Socio

> The vast majority of violent crime in Canada is not committed with a firearm. According to 2006 data reported by police to the UCR Survey, most violent crime (75%) was committed by physical force or threats, without the use of any weapon. Weapons were used against 18% of victims of violent crimes, with knives (6.2%) and clubs or blunt instruments (3.0%) being the most common. A firearm was used against 2.4% of all victims (Table 1).

Comparing Homeschooling vs Public Schooling: Ten Reasons for Homeschooling Children by Joe Puma

> Do you know why students have the summer off? It is so they can work the fields of their family's farm because 90% of people live in farming communities. Wait . . . that statistic is from 1920. These days less than 5% of people live and work on a family farm.

Justice: The Quality of Mercy

> According to Statistics Canada (statcan.gc.ca), there were about "163,000 adult offenders (18 years or over)" in Canada's correctional system in 2010/2011. While

Aboriginal people make up approximately 3% of the Canadian population, statistics show they make up more than 20% of the prison population (Dauvergne, Mia. *Adult Correctional Statistics In Canada, 2010/2011*).

Surveys, interviews, experiments, and personal observations are other fact based forms of evidence.

Analogies

Likening one thing to another is also a persuasive technique. An original and apt analogy is often thought provoking and supportive of your argument. Analogies make abstract ideas tangible.

A Problem with Wind Power by Eric Rosenbloom

It's not like riding a bike and leaving the car in the driveway. Wind energy on the grid is more like riding a bike and having someone follow you in the car in case you get tired.

Food and Wine Pairing is Just a Big Scam by Alder Yarrow

But just like cancers that can grow from seemingly benign cells, these basic sensibilities planted the seeds of a poisonous idea, one that has grown to the point that every evening around the world, wine lovers stand paralyzed in the aisles of grocery stores and in the halls of wine stores, trying desperately to choose the "right" wine for whatever they are making for dinner that night.

Graphics

Presenting evidence graphically reinforces your text and focuses the reader's attention. When there is a combination of text and graphics on a page, we focus first on the graphics. Readers enjoy the immediacy and variety introduced by tables, charts, and infographics.

Firearms and Violent Crime by Mia Dauvergne and Leonardo De Socio

Overall homicide rates are highest in the United States, followed by Canada, Australia, and England and Wales. While non-firearm homicide rates are similar between the four countries, the rates of firearm-related homicides are quite different.

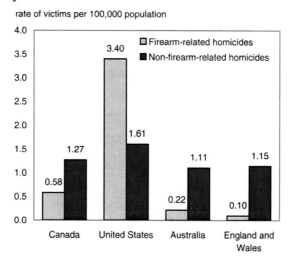

Donuts Versus Muffins At Tim Hortons

Say you are watching your weight but you accidentally wander into a Tim Hortons coffee shop. You might think that having a muffin is a wiser choice than having a donut. However, check out Table One (below) and you might think again.

Table One

	Chocolate Dip Donut	Banana Nut Muffin
Calories	210	390
Total Fat (g)	8	16
Saturated Fat (g)	3.5	2.5
Trans Fat (g)	0	0.2
Cholesterol (mg)	0	35
Sodium (mg)	190	490
Carbohydrates (g)	30	52

	Chocolate Dip Donut	Banana Nut Muffin
Carbs (g)	30	52
Sugars (g)	7	27
Protein (g)	4	6
Data Source: Tim Hortons Nutrition Guide - *timhortons.com*		

The same information presented as an infographic is also interesting and immediate.

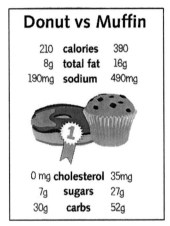

Donut vs Muffin

210	**calories**	390
8g	**total fat**	16g
190mg	**sodium**	490mg

0 mg	**cholesterol**	35mg
7g	**sugars**	27g
30g	**carbs**	52g

Quotations

Writers frequently support their ideas with quotations. Expert opinion and articulate statements are convincing:

Your Rebel Brain by Jeff Wise

> According to Lilianne R. Mujica-Parodi, director of the Laboratory for the Study of Emotion and Cognition at Stony Brook University School of Medicine, "People enjoy taking risks not because they like the excitatory feeling"— the adrenaline rush—"but because they love the feeling afterward," when the body's system for calming itself swings into overdrive.

The Pragmatic Writer

> Writing in their characteristically pithy and balanced

style, Strunk and White remind us that authors should "prefer the specific to the general, the definite to the vague, the concrete to the abstract."

A combination of quotation and paraphrase allows for retaining the voice and authority of the original quotation while summarizing it for the sake of brevity:

The World's Greatest Explorers

> In *Longitude*, Dava Sobel explains that "every great captain in the Age of Exploration became lost at sea" because they could not determine their exact longitude. So, the British government offered a "king's ransom" to the person who could offer a realistic means of determining longitude at sea. Solving the problem "assumed legendary proportions..." (*Longitude: The True Story of a Lone Genius Who Solved the Greatest Scientific Problem of His Time*).

The Happiness Syndrome by Maggie Scarf

> What is the frequency of happiness? Controlled research on the subject is scarce and inconclusive. But, as Bentall argues, uncontrolled observations, such as those found in plays, novels and soap operas, indicate "that happiness is a relatively rare phenomenon." A good amount of data of other kinds (such as informal surveys of one's acquaintances) also gives credibility to Bentall's suggestion that episodes of happiness occur infrequently, and are often of markedly brief duration.

When using quotations and paraphrase, always acknowledge the source.

Trust, Logic, And Passion

Aristotle observed that authors use three principle means of persuasion: they appeal to our sense of trust, our sense of logic, or our emotions. His observation, made several thousand years ago, stands the test of time. The persuasive methods are described below.

Trust

Trust based evidence relies on the credibility and character of the author. The author says to the audience, "Believe me because I have integrity," or "Believe me because I am experienced and qualified."

Clicker Training

> I have been training dogs for 25 years. I have trained guard dogs, service dogs, and show dogs. And I have always used positive reinforcement in the form of a clicker.

Along with sincerity and integrity, writers present reasonableness as a type of character based evidence. The author says, "Trust me; even though I am not an expert, I am a reasonable person."

Justice: The Quality of Mercy

> I am not a lawyer or a judge or a law enforcement officer, but as a man of faith, I know the difference between right and wrong.

Although highly regarded as a scientist, Suzuki appeals to his audience not on the basis of his academic degrees or expertise as an environmentalist, but on his personal integrity, his willingness to share his idyllic rural retreat with modern technology:

The Beauty Of Wind Farms by David Suzuki

> Off the coast of British Columbia in Canada is an island called Quadra, where I have a cabin that is as close to my heart as you can imagine. From my porch on a good day you can see clear across the waters of Georgia Strait to the snowy peaks of the rugged Coast Mountains. It is one of the most beautiful views I have seen. And I would gladly share it with a wind farm.

Trust based evidence depends on persuading your audience that you are worth listening to because of who you are as a person. Trust based evidence appeals to our belief in others.

Logic

Logic based evidence relies on common sense arguments and observations. The author says to the audience, "Believe me because my ideas are reasonable, rational, and full of common sense."

For example, in *How To Write a Bad Resume*, the authors do not use any statistics, charts, tables, or graphs related to writing a resume. They employ rational arguments. They observe that if you are caught lying on your resume, you are not getting the job. They note that using "10 different fonts, in 6 different sizes, and a wild array of bold, italics, small caps, and colors" hurts your chances of getting the job.

Similarly, Matlock does not quote any experts or cite any studies in her discussion of *How To Remember Names*. She relies on reasonable assumptions and observations: "Business referrals, clients, customers, and patients all want to feel significant."

Statistical proof is not always required. Careful and thoughtful reasoning can be persuasive:

What Is Forgiveness? by Hollye Dexter

> Forgiveness is a huge buzzword these days. Everyone says you should do it. Oprah says you should do it. Doctors say you'll be healthier if you do it. Jesus did it on the cross. Stanford University even has a "Forgiveness Project", where researchers say it is a skill that can be learned, a decision you simply make. But I don't see it as a decision any more than falling in love is a decision.
>
> Forgiveness is a spontaneous shift in the heart, and like love, it can't be forced. It is an unwritten contract

between two souls. A door of genuine understanding and remorse must be opened before you can cross the threshold of forgiveness. You can't bang that door down yourself. In other words, forgiveness is not a one-way street.

What is forgiveness? I don't know that I could encapsulate it into simple words. Like love, I know it when I feel it. When it happens, it is a beautiful miracle, like a butterfly landing on my shoulder. But I think it is a different experience for each person.

Logic based evidence depends on persuading your audience that you are worth listening to because your ideas rest on a level-headed foundation of reasonableness. Logic based evidence appeals to common sense.

Passion

Passion based evidence appeals to our emotions. The author says to the audience, "Believe me because it is best for all concerned."

Writers using passion based evidence stir readers' emotions by using evocative language. Compare the following data based and passion based paragraphs discussing literacy:

Literacy - Data Based
Individuals scoring 1 out of 5 on document literacy tests are categorized as belonging to a low literacy group. Individuals scoring 4 or higher on the same tests are categorized as belonging to a high literacy group. According to Statistics Canada, the median household income for individuals in the low literacy group is $30,000.00. The median income for the high literacy group is $90,000.00.

Literacy - Passion Based
Imagine applying for a job when you can't read the application form. Imagine trying to shop for groceries

when you can't read the labels. Imagine telling your children they can't participate in sports because you don't have the money. Literacy is about more than work, and shopping, and income; it is about human dignity.

Passion based evidence depends on persuading your audience that you are worth listening to because you have something important to say about our common humanity. Passion based evidence appeals to the heart.

The various forms of evidence are not incompatible. A single paragraph can contain many different types. In the following passage, the writer starts with a common sense notion followed by an emotional example. Statistics come next, then the appeal, based on the writer's character:

Justice: The Quality of Mercy

We all know the difference between right and wrong. Help others. Do not lie and steal. Stay away from drugs. But Dwayne never had a chance to learn the difference. Born with FAS (fetal alcohol syndrome) in a remote northern community, Dwayne's notions of right and wrong were shaped by his tormentors. Unfortunately, Dwayne's story is not unusual. While aboriginal people make up approximately 3% of the Canadian population, statistics show they make up more than 20% of the prison population (Dauvergne, Mia, *Adult Correctional Statistics In Canada, 2010/2011*).

I am not a lawyer or a judge or a law enforcement officer, but as a social worker with 20 years of experience, as a person with compassion, I know when society has failed the most vulnerable.

Your choice and use of evidence depend on your goals and your understanding of your audience and their expectations. A professor of geography may be less interested in your passion for wind turbines and more interested in your research and documentation skills. An employee who has just suffered a tragic personal loss is not interested in reading emails that quote the collective agreement.

Work with statistics, charts, tables, and infographics. Use examples and anecdotes, similes and metaphors. Make comparisons, explain relationships, categorize, observe, define, and debate. Write with precision and detachment or poetry and passion. But, always keep the promise made in your introduction.

4. Document Your Sources

The level, formality, and presentation of documentation vary according to the demands of your profession and the expectations of your audience.

If you are an academic writer, strict demands exist, and they vary by discipline. The main style guide for English is the *MLA Style Manual*. The *Publication Manual of the American Psychological Association* is more often used in the social sciences.

All the academic style guides dictate rules for formatting your writing and documenting sources. Most of them are complex enough that books have been written as guides to the style guides.

In academic writing, everything is documented. In his thirteen page academic article discussing insects and dreams, Klein has 91 footnotes documenting other articles. Haydn's 20 page article on teaching history has 77 footnotes.

Your ideas carry more weight when you support your statements with references. Writing, "*Many studies* have shown that girls are not as good at math as boys," is not any better than writing, "*In my opinion*, boys are better at math than girls." Phrases such as *many studies*, *recent research*, and *popular opinion* are vague and unconfirmed.

One advantage of documentation is that readers can verify your sources of information and perform further reading and research.

Another advantage is that meticulous documentation prevents plagiarism.

Plagiarism occurs when a writer uses someone else's words or ideas and does not acknowledge the original source. Even a single word might require documentation if the word was used in an atypical and distinctive way in someone else's writing.

Plagiarism is a serious offense. It can lead a student to a failing grade or expulsion. It can lead a professor to being fired and having all degrees revoked. Plagiarism is also a serious offence outside of an academic setting.

The Director Of Education for the Toronto District School Board resigned after being accused of plagiarism. A candidate for President of the United States withdrew his candidacy after allegations of plagiarism appeared in the press.

Whether you are an academic or non-academic writer, you must never take credit for someone else's words or ideas.

> Plagiarism, which is intellectual theft, occurs where an individual submits or presents the oral or written work of another person as his or her own. Scholarship quite properly rests upon examining and referring to the thoughts and writings of others.

> However, when another person's words (i.e. phrases, sentences, or paragraphs), ideas, or entire works are used, the author must be acknowledged in the text, in footnotes, in endnotes, or in another accepted form of academic citation.

> Where direct quotations are made, they must be clearly delineated (for example, within quotation marks or separately indented). Failure to provide proper attribution is plagiarism because it represents someone else's work as one's own.

Plagiarism should not occur in submitted drafts or final works. A student who seeks assistance from a tutor or other scholastic aids must ensure that the work submitted is the student's own. Students are responsible for ensuring that any work submitted does not constitute plagiarism.

Students who are in any doubt as to what constitutes plagiarism should consult their instructor before handing in any assignments. (*UBC Vancouver Academic Calendar 2013/14* calendar.ubc.ca/vancouver, p.26.)

You must acknowledge your source when you use other people's ideas even if you are not quoting their exact words.

Here is the original quotation:

"For lack of a practical method of determining longitude, every great captain in the Age of Exploration became lost at sea despite the best available charts and compasses. . . . As time passed and no method proved successful, the search for a solution to the longitude problem assumed legendary proportions. . . . The British Parliament, in its famed Longitude Act of 1714, set the highest bounty of all, naming a prize equal to a king's ransom (several million dollars in today's currency) for a 'Practical and Useful' means of determining longitude" (Dava Sobel, *Longitude: The True Story of a Lone Genius Who Solved the Greatest Scientific Problem of His Time*).

Here is a paraphrase:

In *Longitude*, Dava Sobel explains that ships' captains could not navigate with any accuracy because they could not determine their exact longitude, so the British government offered a small fortune to the person who could offer a realistic means of determining longitude at sea.

Placing a single distinct word from the original quotation in quotation marks is also correct:

> As Dava Sobel points out in *Longitude*, discovering a realistic means of determining longitude at sea became a "legendary" quest.

Since you never use quotation marks for anything other than direct quotations, the reader understands that a "legendary" quest is a one word quotation and not a special or ironic use of the word legendary.

Not all professions and audiences are equally rigorous about documentation. However, even if footnotes, parenthetical citations, bibliographies, and works cited are not formally required, documenting your information has six distinct advantages:

1. It is a courtesy for your readers.

2. It shows respect for, and a knowledge of, the work of others.

3. It strengthens your argument.

4. It reinforces your image as a trustworthy author.

5. It prevents plagiarism.

6. It promotes further study and research.

Chapter Five Summary - Conduct A Guided Tour

Take your readers by the hand and guide them through your landscape. Use transitional devices, provide evidence, and document your sources.

Cold: What Is A Canadian?

I don't trust any country that looks around a continent and says, "Hey, I'll take the frozen part." – Jon Stewart

Introduction

What word best defines a Canadian? Polite? Bump into a Canadian, spill his coffee, and he will apologize to you. Tolerant? We listen to politicians in both official languages. Inventive? Poutine: a mixture of fries, gravy, and cheese curds. Cold? Voila! Canadians are cold. Not in an emotional sense, but physically. We are freezing; and we love it. We embrace the cold; we shun warmth; we crave the chill. Cold is the Canadian identity. Three examples of 100% Canadian choices prove my point: our choice of sports arenas, our choice of real estate, and our choice of pastimes.

Our Choice of Sports Arenas
Anecdotal evidence, collected by looking out my window, tells me that Canada's most abundant natural resource is winter. Given our northern latitude, you might think Canadians would build warm winter indoor sanctuaries, islands of green in our frozen sea of white. No thanks. We choose the ice arena over the grassy field every single time. Thanks to curling rinks, hockey arenas, and skating ovals, we bring winter indoors even in the middle of winter.

Our Choice of Real Estate
Canada has a multitude of islands. Most of them are in the Arctic. Most of them are covered in snow, ice, and

rock. We like it that way. How about adopting the Turks and Caicos tropical islands as our eleventh province? No thanks. Sure, the islands are in the Bahamas; the official language is English; the average winter temperature is +28°C; and the islands expressed an interest in joining Canada, but we said. . . .

Our Choice of Pastimes
Baseball or hockey? Our choice is clear. No sunny summer afternoons at the outdoor baseball park for us. Canadians opt for indoor hockey in the dead of winter. It is not game day; it is Hockey Night in Canada.

As you write your middle paragraphs, ask yourself this: Am I following the path outlined in my introduction, guiding my readers along the way, and providing appropriate evidence?

SIX
The Conclusion

Create A Satisfying Ending

I tell my students, "Say something!" Don't spend the entire essay carefully proving your point just to poop out at the end. . . .
– Judy Johnson

Satisfying conclusions provide readers with the sense of an inevitable and logical ending. Your audience not only recognizes that the journey is complete, they also perceive that your conclusion relates to, and arrives from, everything preceding it.

Your conclusion completes your writing in at least one of five ways. It restates your key points. It creates a frame. It discusses the overall significance of your ideas. It calls for action. It contains a clincher: a memorable sentence that encapsulates your message.

Because your introduction contains your main idea and your key points, it is the ideal starting point for your conclusion. Refer to it constantly while writing your closing paragraphs. When your conclusion is finished, place it beside your introduction and ask yourself if they are congruent.

Create the sense of an ending by following at least one of these five strategies:

1. Restate Your Key Idea
2. Create A Frame
3. Comment
4. Call For Action
5. Close With A Clincher

In all of the following examples, the subheadings *Introduction* and *Conclusion* have been added for clarity if they were not present in the original. Even if your document has no other subheadings, use a subheading for your conclusion. This creates an unmistakable transition point for your readers.

As is the case with your introduction, the length of your conclusion depends on the overall length of your document.

1. Restate Your Key Idea

Restate or summarize your key idea in your conclusion and leave it at that. Take your introduction and rewrite its key elements using synonyms and variations of words. For example, in the following text, the word *poisoned* becomes *poisonous, health* becomes *unhealthy,* and *toxic* becomes *toxicity.* Working with synonyms, *insolence, intimidation,* and *tyranny* become *disrespect, threatening,* and *oppressing.*

Bullying: The Toxic Workplace

> Introduction
> The Oxford English Dictionary defines bullying as "overbearing insolence; personal intimidation; petty tyranny." When these three forms of bullying occur in the workplace, they create a poisoned environment known as the toxic workplace. This report looks at how the toxic workplace harms employees in terms of physical, mental, and emotional health.

> Conclusion
> Bullying in the workplace creates a poisonous atmosphere. Treating employees with disrespect, threatening them, and oppressing them results in a level of toxicity that is physically, mentally, and emotionally unhealthy.

The Curious Connection Between Insects and Dreams by Barrett A. Klein

> Introduction
> Insects are diverse, resourceful, and resilient, serving as

symbols of everything from beauty [1] and rebirth [2], to pestilence and evil [3]. Insects pollinate or devour crops [4], contribute to [5-7] or wreak havoc on technology [8-10], inspire architecture [11-14] or obliterate it [15,16], and advance human health [4,17-20] or vector disease [21,22]. Insects inhabit nearly every earthly niche but in the deep marine [23], and can be found among, on, and even inside humans [22,24], and thus it is no surprise that insects have also made their way into our dreams.

Conclusion

Insects that are so numerous and successful in our awake state also appear to prosper in our dreams. Insects in dreams are frequently objects of fear and dread, sometimes prompting psychoanalysis and medical investigation. The connection between insects and dreams is not limited to psychoses and nightmares, however. The connection survives in cultural and historical flourishes of dream interpretation, art, music, film, and literary dream sequences, and creative species descriptions. Insects and dreams each affect our daily lives and together have the capacity to inspire us in the most curious of ways.

Google's Three Best Kept Secrets

Introduction

Google™ is the preeminent search engine on the internet. According to statowl.com, it has 80% of the market share. By comparison, its closest competitor has 9%. Google is so popular that its name is also a verb. According to Google, they process more than 100 billion searches a month. But for all its popularity, it has three well-kept secrets. This article describes the power of *scholar.google, images.google,* and *site*: and explains how to use them.

Conclusion
Google™ is the most popular search engine on the net. Google Scholar™ refines your search by seeking out scholarly articles. Google Images™ lets you upload an image file from your computer and search for that image on the internet. Site: restricts your search to a specific website.

2. Create A Frame

Symmetry is satisfying. When you frame your writing, your conclusion echoes the technique used in your introduction. If your introduction contained an anecdote, end with an anecdote. If you started with a quotation, end with a quotation. If you opened with a question, end with an answer.

History in Schools and the Problem of "The Nation" by Terry Haydn

Introduction
This paper considers two questions related to the teaching of history in schools. First, to what extent should school history be based around the teaching of the story of the nation's past? And second, to what extent should the teaching of the national past attempt to present a positive picture of the nation's past, rather than a dispassionately objective and critical one?

Conclusion
A reform of the history curriculum which attempts to revert to basing school history around the idea of transmitting a positive and defined story about the national past, using teacher exposition, rote learning and memorisation as the main teaching approach, may well do more harm than good. A history curriculum which focuses primarily on 'kings and queens', 'Our

Island Story' and (in the words of Richard Evans) 'The wonderfulness of us' [77] as a nation, may not be in the best interests of those on whom it is inflicted.

Self-Worth: The Role of the Family

Introduction

Virginia Satir wrote that "feelings of worth can flourish only in an atmosphere where individual differences are appreciated, mistakes are tolerated, communication is open, and rules are flexible - the kind of atmosphere that is found in a nurturing family." What does a nurturing family look like? Does a model exist that. . . .

Conclusion

Regarding a sense of self-worth, the family plays a monumental role in a child's developmental years. As Satir reminds us, "every word, facial expression, gesture, or action on the part of a parent gives the child some message about self-worth. It is sad that so many parents don't realize what messages they are sending."

Judy Johnson: Writing Conclusions

Judy Johnson is an English instructor at North Island College, British Columbia. When she is not marking papers, she periodically maintains her blog *The Judicator*, sings with a community choir or her *Moody Judes* band, feeds her four cats (and sometimes her five children), and loves her Piano Man.

I tell my students, "Say something!" Don't spend the entire essay carefully proving your point just to poop out at the end with a meaningless restatement of your thesis or introduction––something like, "And so I have proven that the author's imagery and symbolism contributes to the meaning of the text." I tell them that writing the conclusion is probably the hardest part because they are just so done with the essay and feel they have said all they need to say. But they have to push the ideas into and through the conclusion so that their ideas resonate and remain with readers.

---

3. Comment

Writers often comment on the significance of their main idea.

The Mortgage: Till Death Do Us Part

> Introduction
> The word mortgage has its origins in the French words *mort*, as in death, and *gage*, as in pledge. Add to that the Latin root *mortuum vadium*, and the word literally means dead pledge. In spite of the fact that a mortgage seems eternal, the pledge dies in one of two ways: either the debt is repaid, and the obligation is dead, or the borrower defaults, and the deal is dead. Let's talk about killing the obligation.
>
> Conclusion
> We have seen three tactics for dispatching a mortgage in record time. Not everyone will have the resources or the self-discipline required for implementing all the strategies simultaneously. However, even if you implement only one of them, the financial reward is worthwhile.

In the following example, the authors do not reiterate their opening statement that lower tuition fees do not increase enrolment; instead, they comment on the consequences of maintaining low tuition fees.

Would Higher Tuition Fees Restrict Access To University Studies? by Norma Kozhaya and Germain Belzile

> Introduction
> In reality, this debate is based on a false choice. The

available data for the various Canadian provinces show no direct relationship between tuition fee levels and access to university studies. In other words, low tuition fees do not result in high enrolments.

Conclusion
Governments face various pressures in allocating limited resources, particularly with the rapid cost increases in the health care sector. It seems obvious that they cannot continue to finance universities adequately if tuition fees do not follow the growth in costs. Not allowing university tuition fees to rise seriously compromises the quality of higher education in Quebec without benefiting less well-off students. At the end of the day, what does it matter if everyone can attend university when the diplomas they receive are worthless?

4. Call For Action

In some instances, writers call for action.

Food and Wine Pairing is Just a Big Scam by Alder Yarrow

Introduction
Did I just say that? Yes I did. And increasingly I'm hearing it from wine professionals that I know -- spoken, of course, in hushed tones and off the record. Most professional sommeliers and wine writers wouldn't be caught dead uttering such terms in public, let alone publishing them. So I guess it's up to us bloggers to spread the word: wine drinkers around the world, you've been hoodwinked. Tricked. Bamboozled. Conned.

Conclusion
Go forth and break free from your chains. The only answer to what to drink with what you eat is, in the end, everything and anything.

In *How To Remember Things,* Lickerman sums up his 1600 word essay in one paragraph:

Introduction

. . . . The mind's capacity to store and recall information is truly wondrous. Since I attended medical school we've learned a lot about memory and learning. Though much of what follows are techniques I used to survive my first two years of medical school, much of the science that proves they work is new.

Conclusion

If the mind is indeed like a muscle (and research is validating that model more and more) then memory may very well be like muscle tone: the more the mind is used, the more robust memory may become. As I've moved on from my medical school days to reach early (very early) middle age, I've found myself experiencing benign forgetfulness far more than I like. As a result, I find myself comforted that the old adage "use it or lose it" is seeming more and more not just to apply to the body but to the mind as well.

Stereotypes - Five Types of Men

Introduction

I have, unfortunately, dated them all. The man of letters, the tough guy, the banker, the comedian, and the body. They all play their roles well. But they are all stereotypes. I am looking for something different, something genuine. Let me describe the five types of men that do not interest me: the scholar, the redneck, the banker, the goofball, and the body.

Conclusion

Men, here is my advice. Shun the stereotype. Never mind about the roof, the rifle, or the Rottweiler. All we women ask is this: Be honest. Be yourself. Cuddle a little. Talk. Pay for dinner. Show affection in public. Be courteous and thoughtful and respectful and smart. Act with integrity and dress nicely. We do not want a stereotype; we want a man with character.

In *Enbridge Pipe Dreams And Nightmares*, Lee outlines four key areas in his introduction: job creation, alternative investment, value-added production, and economic costs. In his four paragraph conclusion, he calls on the federal and provincial government to take action in all four areas.

Enbridge Pipe Dreams And Nightmares: The Economic Costs And Benefits Of The Proposed Northern Gateway Pipeline by Marc Lee

Introduction
This paper analyzes claims about new job creation from construction and operation of the NGP, but also considers alternative investments that would reduce Canada's reliance on fossil fuels and its greenhouse gas emissions. It also considers value-added production in Canada and domestic energy security as alternative conceptions of Canada's national interest. Finally, it reviews the economic costs associated with adverse environmental impacts — pipeline and tanker spills and greenhouse gas emissions — as a necessary comparison against economic benefits.

Conclusion
While proponents of the northern gateway pipeline have generally stooped to smearing opponents as "radicals" and "puppets of foreign interests," they have offered few strong justifications for the pipeline other than "jobs and growth." But there are good reasons to question both the actual employment gains that would accrue to workers as well as a growth model that threatens oils spills on land and sea, and climate

change impacts.

A full consideration of costs and benefits must be part of the public debate and environmental assessment process of the NEB. When including damages from GHG emissions, and the costs associated with likely oil spills, the NGP may well be uneconomical.

An alternative path lies in green investments in areas like energy efficiency, renewable energy sources, public transit, waste reduction and management, and in protecting existing jobs that rely on healthy watersheds and coastlines in the impacted region. Paying for these investments through a carbon tax or increased corporate taxes, or oil and gas royalties, would create more employment opportunities, while removing dependence on fossil fuels for domestic energy and reducing greenhouse gases.

Such a shift would, of course, require a very different kind of leadership on the part of the federal and provincial governments to make the transition to a sustainable economy a matter of national and provincial urgency. It would elevate climate action from something to be ignored to a national industrial and employment strategy. In the meantime, stopping a pipeline that further locks Canada onto a path of resource extraction and climate disruption is a sensible step toward that goal.

What is Charisma? How To Be Charismatic by Matthew Scott

Introduction
It is common for people to struggle with a definition of 'charisma' in relation to communication and the social sciences. Ultimately charisma is the result of excellent communication or interpersonal skills, as such skills

can be learned and developed - so developing our own charisma is possible. Becoming charismatic involves paying careful attention to how we interact with other people; the traits that make up charisma are positive and appealing to others. The charismatic person uses their skills to get people on their side, perhaps from a professional, ideological or social point of view.

.... Some people are more charismatic than others - we can recognise charisma but what makes it? This article explores some of the traits of the charismatic person and how they may be developed.

Conclusion

A sincere smile, maintaining eye contact, being polite and courteous is a very effective way of getting people on your side. People are much more likely to do things for you if they are treated well and you are nice to them.

Authors often conclude that further analysis or study is required.

The Gendered Brain by Cheryl Bereziuk

Introduction

Reports over the last hundred years have consistently pointed to the fact that the whole brain is larger and heavier in men compared to women. In general, statistics indicate that the male brain is between 8 and 15% larger and heavier than the female brain (Pinel, 1999; Smock, 1999).

One possibility in explaining this finding is that the male brain is larger simply because in general their bodies tend to be larger. If this were the case we might expect then that the male brain should be larger particularly in areas involved in motor control of the body but this simply has not been established. And in fact some reports suggest that when we divide brain size by body size the female brain may have the advantage (Majewska, 1996). Still other reports suggest that the male advantage in terms of overall brain size come not from the neuron cells that make up the cerebral cortex (which is the conscious and thinking part of our brains) but from the supporting glial cells that provide structural support for the neural cells. This suggests that even if the male brain is larger it may not confer any intellectual advantage (Fausto-Sterling, 1992).

Conclusion

In conclusion, I am not suggesting that there are not any sex differences in the structure of the human brain but simply that the research to date on the gross morphological characteristics has proven less than ideal. Much more work needs to be done to replicate results especially using larger sample sizes that would garner more confidence in the data. And perhaps a better place to look for sex differences might be at a molecular level of analysis. Thus, an examination of neurotransmitter ratios or number of synaptic connections may be a better place to look for such differences.

Are Small Classes Better? Understanding Relationships between Class Size, Classroom Processes and Pupils' Learning by David Pedder

Introduction

Useful educational research should focus on factors that significantly influence the quality of classroom teaching and learning. Such research should, furthermore, be responsive to the concerns of teachers and those whom they serve, and should be helpful to policy-makers in their practical decision-making. . . . It seems obvious to many teachers and parents that class size is an important factor influencing the effectiveness of what teachers and pupils are able to do to promote high quality learning.

Politicians in this and other countries therefore come under great pressure to reduce class sizes or at least to prevent them from increasing. The inconsistency of class size research has enabled politicians of different persuasions to select those particular findings which support their preferred policy choices (Blatchford & Martin, 1998). Hence, the Conservative government of the day chose to listen to the former advice while the current Labour government promised to listen to the latter.

Conclusion

Class size research needs to attend to the contexts within which class size variation occurs by investigating the different ways class size interacts with other key variables. Teachers bring different strengths and expertise to the classroom. They teach different subjects and work in contexts of varying levels of resourcing and space. The pupils they teach come to class with different personalities, behavioural and ability characteristics. Taking all these facets of classroom life into account it is unsurprising if we find teachers maximising opportunities for pupils to learn in classes of different size in different ways. We need further research to find out how teachers manage to do this in classes of different size in different primary and secondary school contexts.

5. Close With A Clincher

Some of the most satisfying conclusions create the sense of an ending by making a perceptive observation. A clincher is like a tagline: it extends the meaning of your key idea with a concise and perceptive observation. The clincher is always the last sentence in your document.

Walk Softly: The Hidden Costs of Producing Green Energy

Conclusion

Oil, gas, and coal are finite resources. We pollute the planet as we acquire them and then pollute it again as we use them. Our only choice is developing sustainable and alternative sources of energy such as harnessing the wind. However, we should proceed cautiously with deploying these green technologies on an industrial scale. Even the wind leaves a footprint.

Bailouts: Why Are They Only For The Wealthy?

Conclusion

Curry and Shibut report that the U.S. "savings and loan crisis of the 1980s and early 1990s cost taxpayers approximately $124 billion." According to a 2012 report published by the Canadian Centre for Policy Alternatives, Canada's banks "received $114 billion in cash and loan support from both the U.S. and Canadian governments during the 2008-2010 financial crisis." Bailouts are for the wealthy. The rest of us tread water.

Determination: Going Green Takes A Thick Skin

Conclusion

It is true that some members of my neighbourhood association find the solar panels on my roof and the wind turbine atop my garage less than aesthetically pleasing. They say the panels and blades are ugly; they say I am difficult. I am sorry people feel that way. But I live by a simple philosophy: annoy your neighbours; save the planet.

Using a quotation for your clincher also works well.

Think Twice Before Buying An Extended Warranty for Your New Vehicle

Conclusion

Paying for an extended warranty on a new vehicle is betting against yourself and the vehicle. You are saying, "I'm buying a $35,000.00 vehicle, and I predict it will have problems as soon as the regular warranty expires. So, let me give you an extra $1500.00 up front in case I am right. If the vehicle doesn't break, just keep my money."

Here's a better idea. Take the money you would have spent on an extended warranty and place it in a savings account. When your new car warranty expires, you will have $1500.00 plus interest in the bank for items such as a $200.00 fog lamp or a new windshield, which no warranty covers.

As Oliver Wendell Holmes said, "Put not your trust in money, but put your money in trust."

Chapter Six Summary - Create A Satisfying Ending

Keep your conclusion in harmony with your introduction. Provide a satisfying ending.

Cold: What Is A Canadian?

I don't trust any country that looks around a continent and says, "Hey, I'll take the frozen part." – Jon Stewart

Introduction

What word best defines a Canadian? Polite? Bump into a Canadian, spill his coffee, and he will apologize to you. Tolerant? We listen to politicians in both official languages. Inventive? Poutine: a mixture of fries, gravy, and cheese curds. Cold? Voila! Canadians are cold. Not in an emotional sense, but physically. We are freezing; and we love it. We embrace the cold; we shun warmth; we crave the chill. Cold is the Canadian identity. Three examples of 100% Canadian choices prove my point: our choice of sports arenas, our choice of real estate, and our choice of pastimes.

Conclusion

Cold defines us a nation. Sure, we could lounge in the sun like lizards on a rock and bake our bodies bronze just south of the Tropic of Cancer, but we'd rather freeze our buns off at a bonspiel, slipping and sliding sideways on the curling sheet as we furiously sweep and hurry hard and hurry harder. We could load our bike panniers with sunscreen, straw hats, and flip flops, but instead we keep a snow brush, ice scraper, and set of Canadian Tire jumper cables in the back of the 4x4. We love the cold; that is who we are. Maybe we love it a bit too much.

Does my conclusion follow naturally from everything that precedes it; is it congruent with my introduction; does it create a satisfying ending?

Editing

After You Write

Because they claw at a writer's heart, I will not use the word revision or the word rewrite or even the word proofread. Let us talk instead of editing. In the beginning you were a writer; now you are an editor polishing a manuscript. The process requires three things: time, knowledge, and a checklist.

Time

The more time that passes between the act of writing and the act of editing, the better. Deadlines and procrastination typically make this cooling off period more a dream than a reality. But if you can manage a week, a month, or even a few days, you will discover, with ease, there are many words and sentences worthy of fine tuning.

Knowledge

Even if it were possible, which it is not, reading a book on the rules of grammar and punctuation is not required before editing. Instead, spend your time learning how the misuse of verbs is the leading cause of wordiness and how wordiness is the leading cause of poor writing. Learn how the English language contains only four basic punctuation marks and three basic sentence types. This is the fundamental knowledge that most dramatically improves your editing and writing skills.

Checklist

Checklists appear in space stations, hospital operating rooms, and nuclear power plants because they help people save time, avoid errors, and deal with complex systems. You should have one at your writing desk. The single greatest advantage of a checklist is that it makes you mindful of what is indispensable in your writing and helps you avoid common mistakes.

Conclusion

Editing takes time. As difficult as it is, leave as much time as you can between the initial writing and the final editing. Learn the basics of writing concise, confident, and credible sentences. And use a checklist. Editing is challenging, but the reward is an articulate manuscript.

SEVEN
Write Concise, Confident, And Credible Sentences

A sentence should contain no unnecessary words, a paragraph no unnecessary sentences, for the same reason that a drawing should have no unnecessary lines and a machine no unnecessary parts.
– William Strunk, Jr.

Your writing is your baby. Delivering it to the world, you open yourself to criticism. Imagine someone taking your creation, gently folding back the pages, and saying, "My, that is one ugly baby."

In truth, all writers create a few ugly babies. Wordiness, grammatical errors, and misused words damage a writer's credibility and authority. That is why all good writers edit their work.

"That's our new mission statement."

This section provides eleven rules for writing sentences that are clear, concise, and correct.

1. Avoid *To* Verbs

2. Avoid Too Many Verbs

3. Avoid Contractions

1. Avoid *To* Verbs

The first and most important step towards writing concisely and clearly is removing the word *to* in front of verbs.

Avoiding wordiness is not about counting words; it is about avoiding unnecessary words. The strategy of removing *to* verbs works not because it makes sentences shorter, but because it makes them comprehensible.

Wordiness obscures ideas; conciseness brings clarity.

> The purpose of this report is to look at ways to better market our bicycles and to look at ways to convince people to cycle rather than to drive.

> This report discusses marketing our bicycles and encouraging cycling.

> Our mission statement is to provide parts on time, to guarantee quality, to be of assistance to our customers, to be courteous, and to call on all our staff to act with integrity.

> We provide parts on time, guarantee quality, assist our customers, offer courteous service, and act with integrity.

Writing that is concise and clear communicates in a confident, lively, and unambiguous way. It is convincing.

Start by finding the *to* verbs in your own writing and in other people's writing. Some are obvious:

> to address
> to reveal
> to understand
> to reduce
> to implement
> to motivate
> to summarize

Some are sneakier:

> to better remedy
> to at last prove
> to make better
> to finally resolve
> to ultimately put to rest
> to put it another way

Consider this example:

> Employees will no longer be allowed to use their work email accounts to send emails of a non-work related matter.

Rewrite the sentence without the *to use* and *to send* verbs and it reads as follows:

> Email is for work use only.

Both sentences contain the same message. But when you remove *to use* and *to send*, the message becomes memorable because the sentence is now clear, concise, and confident. The writer appears self-assured and in control.

Removing the *to* verbs usually means rewriting the sentence. This revision strategy is worth the effort because it brings precision and punch to your writing.

> I was trying to suggest in my last email that it would be worthwhile to think about another strategy.

> My last email suggested that thinking about another strategy is worthwhile.

Typically, the *to* verbs are easily pruned:

> We look at how to better market environmentalism and the best ways to convince people to buy into recycling.

> The article discusses marketing environmentalism and encouraging recycling.

> In this essay, I am going to discuss frogs.

> This essay discusses frogs.

> We are pleased to present our findings in the following report.

> This report presents our findings.

> We will then proceed to gather more information before attempting to make a decision.

> We will gather more information before making a decision.

> Commas are used to separate items in a list.

> Commas separate items in a list.

> I think one of the secrets of life is to realistically understand and to wholeheartedly accept who you are and then to use this information to your best advantage.

> One of life's secrets is realistically understanding and wholeheartedly accepting yourself and being smart about it.

> If we desire student behaviour to quickly change, we

need <u>to offer</u> the right rewards.

<u>Offer</u> proper rewards, and student behaviour quickly <u>changes</u>.

Does anyone want <u>to come</u> with me <u>to play</u> some tennis?

Tennis anyone?

Changing a *to* verb to an *ing* verb often solves the problem:

It is one thing <u>to want</u> <u>to start</u> a debate about the future of gun control. It is another thing entirely <u>to pass</u> legislation making the ability <u>to possess</u> and <u>to own</u> guns a legislated right <u>to get</u> the ball rolling.

<u>Starting</u> a legitimate argument about the future of gun control is one thing. <u>Getting</u> the ball rolling by <u>passing</u> legislation that makes gun possession and ownership a legislated right is another thing entirely.

Because they sound and feel right, avoiding to verbs requires diligence and discipline. However, every time you replace a to verb with a single verb, your writing becomes more professional, polished, and powerful:

<u>To make</u> this change we need <u>to have</u> a way <u>to first clarify</u> our overall goal.

<u>Making</u> the change <u>starts</u> with <u>clarifying</u> our goal.

I am here today <u>to talk</u> about the city's plans <u>to build</u> a sewage treatment plant in a residential neighbourhood.

We <u>must stop</u> the city from <u>building</u> a sewage treatment plant in our neighbourhood.

Take care not <u>to get caught</u> up in the details or <u>to try to avoid</u> paying too much when it comes time <u>to decide</u>.

<u>Do not</u> let the details or the idea of overpaying control your decision.

2. Avoid Too Many Verbs

Typically, two or more verbs in a row indicate wordiness. When you see a string of verbs, consider replacing them with a single verb.

> We <u>are pleased</u> <u>to be presenting</u> an exhibition of their paintings.

> We <u>proudly</u> present an exhibition of their paintings.

> Research <u>has been completed</u> that demonstrates global warming is a dangerous threat.

> Research <u>proves</u> that global warming is a threat.

> The authors <u>would suggest</u> that the policy <u>should be</u> changed.

> We <u>recommend</u> changing the policy. Or, <u>change</u> the policy.

Avoiding too many verbs often makes your sentences shorter. But reducing word count is not your objective. Your goal is bringing your writing to life and conveying a clear message. Pruning verbs is a valuable strategy because it lets you see your ideas clearly and express them with conviction.

In the following example, the writer is reassuring an unhappy employee. But the sentence is littered with verb strings and *to* verbs:

> Every effort <u>will be made</u> <u>to keep</u> you in the loop and <u>to provide</u> the support which you deserve.

Remove the excess verbs and the sentence becomes shorter, more convincing, and more compelling:

> We <u>promise</u> you continued support and timely information.

Look for strings of verbs in your own writing. As you rewrite sentences, your documents become shorter. What was once 1000 words might become 750 words. Removing deadwood creates space for a more thoughtful and meaningful message:

> Original (19 words): Every effort <u>will be made</u> <u>to keep</u> you in the loop and <u>to provide</u> the support which you deserve.

> Revised (18 words): We <u>promise</u> you continued support and timely information because we <u>respect</u> you and <u>value</u> your years of service.

> Original (58 words): Sometimes it takes so little <u>to really confuse</u> readers that if the author <u>has made</u> a decision to use one wrong word, the reader tends <u>to get lost</u>. So, in this lesson we <u>are going to work</u> on some things <u>to avoid that</u>. The point is <u>to be</u> careful <u>to choose</u> the right word by using a thesaurus.

> Revised (23 words): If the author <u>chooses</u> the wrong word, sometimes it <u>confuses</u> readers. This lesson <u>explains</u> how

you choose the right word using a thesaurus.

Sentences containing strings of verb and *to* verbs are often passive and distant sounding. Removing unnecessary verbs makes sentences more active and immediate. The writing springs to life.

"In this manual <u>we will look</u> at what plagiarism is, how it <u>can hurt</u> you, and how <u>to go</u> about avoiding it."

This manual <u>defines</u> plagiarism, <u>outlines</u> its dangers, and <u>explains</u> proper documentation procedures.

We <u>have been trying</u> unsuccessfully <u>to fill</u> these positions.

We <u>cannot</u> fill these positions.

The building <u>has been redesigned</u> <u>to accommodate</u> same-sex bathrooms.

The new design <u>includes</u> same-sex bathrooms.

We <u>have been trying</u> <u>to be</u> innovative in order <u>to find</u> a good solution that <u>will make</u> everyone happy.

We <u>need</u> an innovative and universal solution.

The Band <u>has been formed</u> by the amalgamation of young, old, and middle age musicians.

The Band <u>is</u> an amalgamation of young, old, and middle age musicians.

It is imperative that we <u>will establish</u> the structures and systems which <u>will allow</u> us <u>to embrace</u> change and <u>to keep</u> responding as the growth within the city dictates.

As the city <u>grows</u>, we <u>grow</u>, but only if we <u>embrace</u> change and <u>establish</u> responsive systems.

The steady evolution of social media <u>has allowed</u> some users not only <u>to find</u> good information to the situation they are in, but <u>to contribute</u> to it as well.

Social media <u>provides</u> new ways of accessing and contributing to the flow of information.

Placing events in the past or future may require using two verbs. But even past events may benefit from replacing strings of verbs with single verbs.

I <u>have been working</u> very hard.

I always <u>work</u> hard.

We <u>are going</u> to <u>try</u> to <u>solve</u> the problem.

Problem solving <u>is</u> the answer.

3. Avoid Contractions

Is it *it's* or *its*? Is a possessive the same as an apostrophe? Did *it's* door fall off, or did *its* door fall off, or did *its'* door fall off?

Unless you are reporting dialogue or writing fiction or writing a letter to your mom, avoid common grammatical errors by avoiding contractions.

Write *it is* instead of *it's*, *do not* instead of *don't*, *she will* instead of *she'll*.

Along with creating grammatical errors, some contractions create unintentional visual oddities:

He will becomes *he'll* which looks like *hell*.

We will becomes *we'll* which looks like *well*.

I'll looks like *ill*.

Who are becomes *who're*.

If you never use contractions, you will never confuse *your* with *you're* or *it's* with *its*:

The car's door fell off. (Correct)

It's door fell off. (Wrong. This means, *it is* door fell off.)

Its' door fell off. (Wrong. There is no such word as *its'*.)

Its door fell off. (Correct)

Like many possessive pronouns, *its* does not have an apostrophe. Think of the other possessive pronouns you know so well: yours, his, hers, ours, theirs, and add *its* to the list.

Contractions appear in practically every form of writing. Writers use them because they make writing seem conversational, less formal, less stiff. But writing is more formal than a conversation, and it is permanent, so avoiding contractions is both appropriate and desirable.

By not using contractions, you may discover a more articulate way of making your point. Contractions often facilitate wordiness:

> They're happy to know that you're actually going to help those who're in need.

> They are happy to know that you are actually going to help those who are in need.

> It makes them happy when you help the needy.

Contractions are not mandatory. Save the apostrophe for showing possession, ownership.

When it comes to contractions, the rule is straightforward: don't use 'em.

4. Consider Ownership

Ownership takes two forms in writing: possession and quotation.

Possession And The Apostrophe

Since you are not using contractions, showing possession is the only reason for using an apostrophe.

All possessives are formed by adding an apostrophe at the end of the word.

> The wind turbine's blade fell off. Its design was faulty.

> The essay's introduction is well written.

The <u>dog's</u> leg healed perfectly.

The <u>report's</u> conclusion is brilliant.

The <u>reports'</u> conclusions are brilliant.

When it comes to possessives, add an apostrophe s (*'s*) at the end of the word. If the word already ends in an s, just add an apostrophe (*'*).

the <u>memo's</u> subject line (referring to one memo)

the <u>memos'</u> subject lines (referring to several memos)

the <u>employee's</u> bonuses (referring to one lucky employee)

the <u>employees'</u> bonuses (referring to several employees)

The trick with possessives is identifying the root word, the word that precedes the ' or the 's. In these examples, as the root word changes from the singular *boy* to the plural *boys*, the meaning changes:

the <u>boy's</u> bike (singular: one boy owns one bike)

the <u>boy's</u> bikes (singular: one lucky boy owns several bikes)

the <u>boys'</u> bike (plural: several boys share one bike)

the <u>boys'</u> bikes (plural: several boys own several bikes)

While all nouns accept an apostrophe, these possessive pronouns do not: yours, his, hers, ours, theirs, and its. For example, the words *our's* and *its'* do not exist.

However, other pronouns use the apostrophe when expressing ownership. They are the *one* words and the *body* words. As long as you are not using contractions, trust your ear; you have heard them used many times.

Why does one boy own so many bikes? It is <u>anyone's</u> guess.

Sharing a bike is <u>nobody's</u> idea of a good time.

Same sex bathrooms was <u>someone's</u> brilliant idea.

Who left the bike in the driveway? It could be <u>anybody's</u>.

<u>Somebody's</u> report is two weeks overdue!

It is no <u>one's</u> fault.

<u>Everyone's</u> cell phone uses a battery.

The problem is not mine; it is <u>everybody's</u>.

One person's idea of a good time is not the same as another <u>one's</u>.

Two other common pronouns taking an apostrophe are *other* and *else*.

We share each <u>other's</u> passion for watching movies.

If you like the idea, it is mine. If you do not like the idea, it is <u>someone else's</u>.

Here is a recap of the rules for creating possessives:

1. Think about who owns it, the *boy* or the *boys*, then place an 's or an ' at the end. reverse ' other direction

2. Do not use an apostrophe with yours, his, hers, ours, theirs, and its.

3. If required, use an apostrophe with the *one* words and the *body* words.

4. Trusting your ear when using the apostrophe works, but only if you never use contractions.

Ownership And Quotation Marks

The humble ' is versatile. As an apostrophe, it shows possession; doubled up it is a quotation mark; used within a quotation, it is a single quotation mark. And, in some writing, it forms those troublesome contractions.

Quotation marks " " show that the words on the page are not yours but someone else's. Here is a quotation from *Nonsense Novels* by the

Canadian humorist Stephen Leacock:

> Lord Ronald said nothing; he flung himself from the room, flung himself upon his horse and rode madly off in all directions.

Here are several ways of using the quotation:

> Leacock provides a perfect description of our safety committee meeting: we met for exactly five minutes before we "rode madly off in all directions."

> Like Leacock's Lord Randall, he "said nothing . . . [and then] rode madly off in all directions."

> I am so disorganized I feel as though I am riding "madly off in all directions."

When you use a quotation within a quotation, the versatile ' becomes a single quotation mark:

> "The Lord said 'Let there be wheat,' and Saskatchewan was born" (Stephen Leacock).

Whenever you use another person's words, you must enclose those words in quotation marks. This is not courteous; it is mandatory.

If you present other people's words as though they were your own, you are guilty of plagiarism. In academic circles the penalties for plagiarism include a failing grade for the assignment or the entire course as well as the possibility of being expelled from school or losing a degree.

Use quotation marks and give credit where it is due. It shows you are reading, thinking, and acknowledging other people's ideas, and those are signs of a sophisticated writer.

Never use quotation marks, double or single, as an indicator that a word or phrase is used in an ironic or special manner or as a means of drawing attention to a word. These are also known as scare quotes or air quotes.

In the following examples, the problem with using quotation marks is that you are not quoting anyone; the reader must guess at your meaning. This makes the quotation marks, double or single, meaningless.

> Nanotubes have "unusual" properties.

> The observed behaviour was not "normal."

> She was 'happy' with the board's decision.

> An engineer's 'mistake' resulted in the collapse of the bridge.

Instead of making the reader guess, explain the special meaning, find the precise word, or rewrite the sentence.

> Nanotubes are light and strong and woven into fabric.

> The observed behaviour was not consistent with all the previous observations.

> She was profoundly frustrated by the board's decision.

> A mathematical miscalculation by an engineer resulted in the collapse of the bridge.

Use single or double quotations marks only when quoting someone's words.

Paraphrase And Individual Words

When you paraphrase someone else's writing, you summarize their ideas in your own words. You always credit the author, but quotation marks are not used as long as you do not quote short phrases, key individual words, or individual words that the author used in a surprising or distinctive manner.

Here is the original quotation from Restak's article *The Other Difference Between Boys and Girls*.

> Girls can sing in tune at an earlier age [than boys]. In fact, if we think of the throat as muscles of fine

control—those in which girls excel—then it should come as no surprise that girls exceed boys in language abilities. . . . Girls read sooner, learn foreign languages more easily, and, as a result, are more likely to enter occupations involving language mastery.

Here is a paraphrase:

In *The Other Difference Between Boys and Girls*, Restak states that when it comes to language skills, girls are superior to boys.

In the original quotation, the words *language, girls,* and *boys* are not used in an unusual or distinguishing manner, so the paraphrase does not require quotations marks.

However, if you use a short phrase from the original, enclose the phrase in quotations marks:

Restak argues that when it comes to "language abilities," girls are superior to boys. As a result, girls often choose careers that involve "language mastery."

When a single word is central to the author's argument, use quotation marks around the word in your paraphrase:

In *The Other Difference Between Boys and Girls*, Restak states that when it comes to language "mastery," girls are superior to boys.

Because single or double quotation marks only signal a direct quotation, readers understand that "mastery" is a one word quotation that appears in Restak's article.

5. Write In The Plural Voice

Using words and phrases that are not offensive or discriminatory is mandatory in all forms of writing. We use gender neutral words such as *firefighter* instead of *fireman* and *letter carrier* instead of *mailman*.

But a common error occurs when we start with a gender neutral word and then make it gender specific:

> When a <u>scientist</u> uses graphs, <u>he</u> must use them sparingly in <u>his</u> presentations.

Since not all scientists are men, writers strive for gender neutrality by using the awkward *he/she* or *he or she* construction.

> When a <u>scientist</u> uses graphs, <u>he/she</u> must use them sparingly in <u>his/her</u> presentations.

> When a <u>scientist</u> uses graphs, <u>he or she</u> must use them sparingly in <u>his or her</u> presentations.

Writing in the plural voice removes the awkwardness and is gender neutral:

> When <u>scientists</u> use adjectives, <u>they</u> must use them sparingly in <u>their</u> presentations.

Writing in the plural voice is easy; just think of many instead of one.

When writing about a specific person, gender specific language is appropriate:

> Marie Curie dedicated <u>her</u> life to science. <u>She</u> won two Nobel prizes.

6. Think In Terms Of Periods And Commas

When it comes to punctuating sentences, think in terms of periods and commas. If any punctuation mark contains a period, it means come to a full stop. A comma means pause.

The Period

Use the period, and any punctuation mark containing a period, only at the end of a sentence. A sentence is a complete thought, a fully stated idea. Your ear tells you the following statements are not sentences because the ideas are incomplete:

If the lock is changed.

As one of the world's fastest growing companies.

The rules are.

For example.

The most important fact is.

Even though the above statements end with a period, they are partial, incomplete, thoughts; they leave the reader hanging because they are fragments of ideas.

A period indicates the end of a complete thought. Like a red light or a stop sign at an intersection, the period says to the reader, "Come to a full stop."

Four familiar punctuation marks include the period:

! Exclamation Mark

? Question Mark

: Colon

; Semicolon

If the punctuation mark contains a period, use it only at the end of a sentence, at the end of a completed thought.

I have an essay due on Monday.

I have a report due on Tuesday!

I have an essay due on Monday?

I have an essay due on Monday; I have a report due on Tuesday.

I have an essay due on Monday: I have a report due on Tuesday.

The Semicolon

Because the semicolon contains a period, we follow the rule and only use it at the end of a thought that stands on its own.

"Can anyone, *anyone*, tell me how a semicolon is used other than in emoticons?!"

Information technology dominates the world. It is ubiquitous.

Information technology dominates the world; it is ubiquitous.

Prior to 1990, rifles/shotguns were used far more frequently than handguns; however, in 1991, the use of handguns surpassed rifles/shotguns for the first time (Mia Dauvergne).

Becoming charismatic involves paying careful attention to how we interact with other people; the traits that make up charisma are positive and appealing to others (Matthew Scott).

When discussing cause and effect, ask yourself three questions: did A cause B; or, did B cause A; or, were A and B caused by C?

We don't merely desire love, truth, goodness, beauty,

and unity; we want all of these things in their ultimate, perfect, never-ending form (John Keenan).

The Colon

The colon consists of two periods; therefore, the colon marks the end of a sentence. Typically, the colon introduces a list or an example.

Consider the following examples of illegal use of the colon.

The art gallery committee now includes: the mayor, the gallery manager, and the treasurer. (Wrong)

Wind turbines are environmentally friendly. For example: they use a renewable energy source, they use a minimal amount of land, and they last forever. (Wrong)

My three goals are: to become a better writer, to avoid the use of the to verb construction, and to learn how to avoid contractions. (Wrong)

Isolate the statements in front of the colon in the above examples. They are not complete sentences.

The art gallery committee now includes:

For example:

My three goals are:

The following are complete sentences:

The art gallery committee now includes three people.

The art gallery committee now includes the mayor, the gallery manager, and the treasurer.

For example, wind turbines use a renewable energy source, they use a minimal amount of land, and they last forever.

My three goals are to become a better writer, to avoid the use of the to verb construction, and to learn how to avoid contractions.

Or, let the colon introduce the list.

> <u>The art gallery committee now</u> includes three people: the mayor, the gallery manager, and the treasurer.

> Wind turbines are environmentally friendly: they use a renewable energy source, they use a minimal amount of land, and they last forever.

> <u>I have three goals:</u> become a better writer, avoid the use of the *to* verb construction, and avoid contractions.

The statement preceding the colon must form a sentence, a group of words that stand on their own.

If the punctuation mark contains a period, it needs a complete thought in front of it.

The Comma

The period is a full stop; the comma is a pause. Periods prevent collision between sentences: commas prevent collisions within sentences.

Commas separate items in a list.

> Victor Borge was a comedian, a pianist, and a conductor.

Commas also separate words and phrases in a sentence. The natural order of a sentence is that someone does something, and then the details follow.

> Jack ran from the tax collector.

When the natural order is interrupted by details, commas are required.

> Jack<u>, who was out on parole,</u> ran from the tax collector.

> Few people<u>, for example,</u> have a difficult time remembering the names of people they find attractive (Lickerman).

Canadians, however, must appreciate that just saying that Canada is a multicultural society is not enough (Ravelli).

When the natural order is reversed (when the details come first), a comma is required.

From the tax collector, Jack ran.

A complex set of rules is not required. Your ear tells you when the natural sentence order, the basic sentence, is inverted or interrupted. Commas separate, identify, and acknowledge the details that interrupt the natural order of the sentence.

Here is an expression of a complete thought:

Victor Borge was a famous musician and a poultry farmer.

If you interrupt the natural order of the sentence with a word or a phrase, separate the word or phrase with commas.

Victor Borge was, even though few people know it, a famous musician and a poultry farmer.

Victor Borge was, surprisingly, a famous musician and a poultry farmer.

Victor Borge, the famous musician, was also a poultry farmer.

If you reverse the natural order of the sentence by placing a word or a phrase before the basic sentence, separate the word or phrase with a comma.

Surprisingly, Victor Borge was also a poultry farmer.

Even though few people know it, Victor Borge, the famous musician, was also a poultry farmer.

Warning: There are two inherent comma hazards. The first is joining two sentences with a comma instead of separating them with a period.

I phoned in sick today, I will be in tomorrow. (Wrong)

I phoned in sick today. I will be in tomorrow. (Correct)

I phoned in sick today, but I will be in tomorrow. (Correct)

The second hazard is punctuating with commas according to the rhythms of speech rather than the rules of grammar:

I want to be perfectly clear that I had, no idea, what my accountant was doing. (Wrong)

It is as though the writer thinks, "I need emphasis on the phrase *no idea,* so I will highlight the phrase by surrounding it with commas and slowing down the reader. However, never use commas for emphasis or dramatic breaks.

Commas also introduce direct quotations when the quotation is preceded by an incomplete sentence:

<u>The same article stated,</u> "The government paid consultants $11.8 million, or $90,000 a day, to suggest ways to trim budgets."

<u>A spokesperson for the restaurant said,</u> "We're now opening a store, a full service store, every other day."

However, if the word *that* precedes the quotation, do not use a comma:

<u>The same article stated that</u> "The government paid consultants $11.8 million, or $90,000 a day, to suggest ways to trim budgets."

<u>A spokesperson for the restaurant said that</u> "We're now opening a store, a full service store, every other day."

When placing a comma, ask yourself three questions:

1. Am I separating items in a list?

2. Have I inverted or interrupted my basic sentence?

3. Does an incomplete sentence precede the quotation?

Special Cases: Leaving Words Out And Adding Words

The only time the period does not indicate a full stop, a complete thought, is when it is used as an ellipsis . . . three evenly spaced periods.

When ellipses appear in a quotation, they indicate that words have been omitted from the original.

Here is a quotation from *Does Studying Behavioral Economics Improve Your Financial Decisions?* by Sam McNerney:

> Taleb's position is that when it comes to deciding rationally, our brains just aren't up for the task. True, humans have the most sophisticated minds on the planet. But the mental mechanisms that biologically separate us from other species, those cognitive parts which permit us to assess the pros and cons of buying a stereo, new cars, or theater tickets are brand new; and like any first generation technology, they are prone to several systematic errors. As Jonah Lehrer says, "when it comes to the new parts of the brain, evolution just hasn't had time to work out the kinks."

Here is the quotation shortened by using ellipses:

> Taleb's position is that . . . our brains just aren't up for the task. True, humans have the most sophisticated minds on the planet. But the mental mechanisms that biologically separate us from other species . . . are brand new; and . . . they are prone to several systematic errors.

When the ellipsis appears at the end of a sentence, add a period:

> Taleb's position is that when it comes to deciding rationally, our brains just aren't up for the task. True, humans have the most sophisticated minds on the planet. But the mental mechanisms that biologically

> separate us from other species, those cognitive parts
> which permit us to assess the pros and cons of buying
> a stereo, new cars, or theater tickets are brand new....

When adding words to a quotation for clarity or comment, place the words in square brackets [ ].

> FPL Energy also says, "although construction is temporary [a few months], it will require heavy equipment, including bulldozers, graders, trenching machines, concrete trucks, flatbed trucks, and large cranes."

> Indeed, new turbines may have quieter bearings and gears, but the huge magnetized generators can not avoid producing a low-frequency hum, and the problem of 100-foot rotor blades chopping through the air at over 100 mph also is insurmountable (a 35meter [115-foot] blade turning at 15 rpm is travelling 123 mph at the tip, at 20 rpm 164 mph). Every time each rotor passes the tower, the compression of air produces a deep resonating thump (Eric Rosenbloom).

Special Cases: Dashes And Parenthesis

In *The Elements of Style*, Strunk and White write that a "dash is a mark of separation stronger than a comma, less formal than a colon, and more relaxed than parentheses. ... Use a dash only when more common marks of punctuation seem inadequate."

Dashes are not illegal, but they are tricky. Simplify your writing life by using commas instead.

Parentheses (also known as brackets) have several functions. First of all, they function as giant commas and separate details that interrupt the natural order of the sentence:

> John F. Kennedy (35th President of the United States) said, "Ask not what your country can do for you; ask

what you can do for your country." (Correct)

John F. Kennedy, 35th President of the United States, said, "Ask not what your country can do for you; ask what you can do for your country." (Correct)

When buying a used car, remember the Latin saying "caveat emptor" (buyer beware). (Correct)

When buying a used car, remember the Latin saying "caveat emptor," buyer beware. (Correct)

Parentheses also identify the source of quotations.

"Nor will any amount of disturbance of the ordinary rules of grammar, the freedom called 'poetic license,' in and of itself make poetry, any more than a liquor license can make liquor" (Stephen Leacock, *How to Write*).

Punctuation Summary

1. If a punctuation mark contains a period (; : ? !), it must appear at the end of a sentence; a sentence is a complete thought that stands on its own.

2. Commas separate items in a list.

3. Commas clarify inverted and interrupted sentences.

4. Commas introduce a quotation prefaced by an incomplete sentence.

5. The ellipsis . . . indicates omitted words within quotations.

6. Within quotations, square brackets indicate added words.

7. Parentheses (also called brackets) function much like overgrown commas.

7. Use Three Sentence Types

Writers use only three sentence types because only three sentences types exist: Simple, Compound, and Complex.

Everything written in English, *The Bible*, *The National Enquirer*, the complete works of Shakespeare, *People* magazine, and the novels of Stephen King, uses only these three types.

A simple sentence is a single, complete, stand-alone thought. It contains one main idea.

A compound sentence contains two main ideas. A compound sentence is two simple sentences, two complete thoughts, combined into one sentence.

A complex sentence is one complete thought and one incomplete thought combined into one sentence.

> One Complete Thought = One Simple Sentence
>
> One Complete Thought + One Complete Thought = One Compound Sentence
>
> One Complete Thought + One Incomplete Thought = One Complex Sentence

Simple sentences are straightforward. But you cannot write everything in simple sentences or everything sounds like a Grade One reader.

Variety, sophistication, and clarity all derive from mastering sentence types. And sentence types are all about combination techniques, transitional words, and making sense.

Simple Sentences: Making Sense

A simple sentence contains one main idea. A main idea is one complete and independent thought. You recognize a complete thought when the sentence makes sense by itself. A simple sentence stands on its own.

> Today's job market is more challenging than ever before (Basham and Sarkesian).

A sentence begins with a capital and ends with a period. But, the true test of a sentence is whether or not it makes sense when removed from the sentences surrounding it. It must be coherent even when taken out of context:

> We must not allow other people's limited perceptions to define us (Virginia Satir).

> The song *Crazy*, by Gnarls Barkley, borrows its bass line from the soundtrack of a 1968 film.

> A basic home brewing kit at MoreBeer.com costs $109 (Julia Scott).

> Do you know why students have the summer off? (Joe Puma).

> Elvis Presley never won an Oscar.

Even without any context, the above sentences make sense. Imagine you are walking down the street and a sinister-looking stranger approaches you and says, "I didn't see nothing."

As you dial 911, you might observe that, even though the stranger is scary and using a double negative, at least the sentence is comprehensible. You have no context, but you still understand what the person means.

If your idea starts with a capital and ends with a period, it must be comprehensible on its own. The basic meaning of a simple sentence is independent of the sentences surrounding it.

Transitional Words And Simple Sentences

Transitional words make sentences flow by linking related ideas.

A specific set of words exists for creating transitions between simple sentences. Below is a partial list of transitional words and phrases used in simple sentences.

The words in the following list are not chosen at random. They are a special group of words used with simple sentences. Keep the list handy when writing or search the internet for *transitional words*.

Transitional Words Used In Simple Sentences

and	as a result	in addition
but	additionally	in contrast
or	accordingly	moreover
nor	consequently	nevertheless
for	furthermore	nonetheless
yet	for example	similarly
so	however	therefore

If the above words or phrases start a simple sentence, they are followed by a comma. If the words or phrases interrupt the natural flow of the sentence, by appearing in the middle, they are surrounded by commas.

All of the following examples are simple sentences using transitional words.

In addition, sour gas wells are life threatening.

Therefore, we objected to sour gas wells being drilled near our home.

However, the drilling company ignored us.

Furthermore, they rejected all our safety and environmental concerns.

The area is, for example, a designated marshland.

Arbitration was, however, not a possibility.

They responded, moreover, by beginning drilling operations immediately.

Compound Sentences: Transitional Words And Connection Techniques

A compound sentence contains two main ideas because it consists of two simple sentences bolted together. Here are two simple sentences:

A tomato is a fruit. A peanut is a legume.

Once combined, the two simples become compound sentences. Please note the punctuation:

A tomato is a fruit, and a peanut is a legume.

A tomato is a fruit; a peanut is a legume.

A tomato is a fruit; furthermore, a peanut is a legume.

A tomato is a fruit: a peanut is a legume.

Like simple sentences, compound sentences begin with a capital and end with a period. Simple sentences become compound sentences by following a simple and precise set of punctuation rules. Fortunately, there are only four rules.

Rule One

Connect two simple sentences using a comma and a transitional word. When forming a compound sentence, there are only seven words that accept a comma. Note that the comma appears in front of the word.

Transitional Words That Connect Using A Comma

, and	, for
, but	, yet
, or	, so
, nor	

Think of the comma and the transitional word as a nut and bolt.

Kopi Luwak coffee comes from animal scat. It is very expensive.

Kopi Luwak coffee comes from animal scat, so it is very expensive.

New Zealand has a population of about 4.5 million people. It has a population of about 40 million sheep.

New Zealand has a population of about 4.5 million people, and it has a population of about 40 million sheep.

Some people believe that licking your elbow is impossible.
I can lick my elbow.

Some people believe that licking your elbow is
impossible,_but_ I can lick my elbow.

Connecting two simple sentences requires both the nut and the bolt.
If you only use the comma, and leave out the word *and*, you create
two simple sentences that run into each other:

A tomato is a fruit, a peanut is a legume. (Wrong)

If you only use the word *and*, and leave out the comma, you also create
a sentence fragment.

A tomato is a fruit and a peanut is a legume. (Wrong)

Used with the comma at the end of a complete thought, the words *and,
but, or, nor, for, yet,* and *so* provide the reader with two key signals:

1. A new complete thought is on the way.

2. Here is the direction of the thought.

    I like you,_and_ I like your sister.
    (Headed in the same direction)

    I like you,_but_ I do not like your cat.
    (Headed in a different direction)

    I like you,_or_ maybe it is your car I like.
    (Headed in either direction)

    I like you,_yet_ I also like your sister.
    (Headed for trouble)

Rule Two

Connect two simple sentences using a semicolon without any
transitional word; this works because the semicolon has a period in it.

Avery Ann is an honours student; she is also class
president.

"Knowledge is knowing a tomato is a fruit; wisdom is

not putting it in a fruit salad" (Anonymous).

Shakespeare was a literary genius; his plays explore the full range of the human experience.

The residents have no evacuation route; this is unacceptable.

This is an easy rule. But why use a semicolon instead of a comma and a transitional word?

The semicolon tells the reader that the ideas are so closely connected that a transitional word is not required. The ideas are so strongly linked that they belong as physically close together on the page as possible.

Using only the semicolon also adds variety to your writing and demonstrates an agreeable level of style and sophistication:

> Another time, we threw a party at which a somewhat plastered guest overturned a punch bowl . . .; two couples left with the wrong spouses; several noisy quarrels broke out; and the hostess seriously considered leaving and staying with our next-door neighbors. . . (Scarf).

Rule Three

Join two simple sentences using a colon. This works because the colon has two periods in it and always appears at the end of a complete thought.

> You are never too old: Roget was seventy three when he published *Roget's Thesaurus*.

> The Nobel Peace Prize medal shows Alfred Nobel on the front: the back of the medal depicts three naked men.

> The Governor General's salary was $137,500.00 in 2012: in 2013 the salary increased to $270,602.00.

Like the semicolon, the colon lends an air of sophistication. It also signals the reader that the two ideas are emphatically linked. Everyone uses the colon at the start of a list: good writers use it between two complete sentences; the best writers use it sparingly.

Rule Four

Connect two simple sentences using a semicolon, a transitional word, and a comma. Think of this splicing device as a nut, a bolt, and a washer.

The same transitional words used in simple sentences also appear in compound sentences. However, the punctuation is different. Here is a partial list of words and phrases used in compound sentences.

Transitional Words That Connect Sentences Using A Semicolon And A Comma

; as a result,	; in addition,
; additionally,	; in contrast,
; accordingly,	; moreover,
; consequently,	; nevertheless,
; furthermore,	; nonetheless,
; for example,	; similarly,
; however,	; therefore,

Kopi Luwak coffee comes from animal scat; therefore, it is very expensive.

New Zealand has a population of about 4.5 million people; in addition, it has a population of about 40 million sheep.

Some people believe that licking your elbow is impossible; however, I can lick my elbow.

Here are three simple sentences:

Music is based on mathematical relationships.

There are eight notes in a major scale.

There are twelve semitones in a major scale.

They remain simple sentences even as you add transitional words and commas:

> Furthermore, music is based on mathematical relationships.

> A major scale, for example, consists of eight notes.

> There are, in addition, twelve semitones in a major scale.

When two sentences are merged and become a compound sentence, commas are not sufficient; in this case, compound sentences demand semicolons.

> Music is based on mathematical relationships; for example, a major scale consists of eight notes.

> A major scale, for example, consists of eight notes; in addition, there are twelve semitones in a major scale.

> Music is based on mathematical relationships; for example, there are eight notes in a major scale; in addition, there are twelve semitones in a major scale.

Punctuation marks are signposts. The semicolon and colon say to the reader, "Look how closely related these ideas are." The semicolon, transitional word, and comma say to the reader, "Slow down and consider the relationship between the ideas."

Each connection technique has its own speed, tone, and message.

> I like wine. I love chocolate.

These two simple sentences come across as plain statements of fact with a big pause, a full stop, between them. When joined with a comma and a transitional word, the connection between the sentences becomes clear; the ideas flow more quickly.

Readers breeze past the comma, which signals a slight pause. And, they also skim over the short transitional word. In the following compound sentence, the writer declares a clear preference for chocolate and drops a hint for the perfect Valentine's Day gift:

I like wine, but I love chocolate.

Written with a different transitional word, the writer indicates that both wine and chocolate make wonderful gifts:

I like wine, and I love chocolate.

With a semicolon, the ideas are pulled together, but the writer suggests, rather than states, that both wine and chocolate make fine gifts. As is the case with two simple sentences, we still see a full stop, but the semicolon does not slow the reader down as much two simple sentences do:

I like wine; I love chocolate.

When you use the semicolon, a large transitional word, and a comma, you flag the reader over to the side of the road and say, "Hey, take a look at where this idea is headed."

I like wine; however, I love chocolate.

Punctuation controls rhythm, pace, and meaning.

Complex Sentences: Transitional Words And Demotion Techniques

Simple and Compound sentences deal with complete thoughts. A simple sentence is a complete thought; a compound sentence is two complete thoughts. However, the complex sentence consists of a complete thought and an incomplete thought.

Just as there is a specific list of words used in simple and compound sentences, there is a precise list of words used in complex sentences.

Here is a partial list of words and phrases used in complex sentences.

Transitional Words That Subordinate And Demote Ideas

after	even though	while
although	if	when

because	once	whether
before	since	
even if	unless	

The technical term for these words is *subordinate conjunction*. This is an apt term because they demote, or subordinate, an idea. Take any simple sentence and place one of the above words or phrases at the start or the end of the sentence, and you turn a complete thought, a simple sentence, into an incomplete thought:

Henry Ford built a town in the Amazon jungle. (Correct)

It was a failure. (Correct)

If Henry Ford built a town in the Amazon jungle. (Wrong)

Because Henry Ford built a town in the Amazon jungle. (Wrong)

It was a failure *because.* (Wrong)

Since it was a failure. (Wrong)

Incomplete thoughts are easily recognized; they begin with a specific transitional word; they leave you hanging; they do not stand on their own; they leave you saying, "Huh?"

Because he also wrote humorous novels and short stories. (Wrong)

If he did not descend immediately. (Wrong)

Since they worked a statutory holiday. (Wrong)

The incomplete thoughts shown above require a complete thought before they make sense. In the following examples, the complete thought is underlined:

Because he is famous for his humorous novels and short stories, <u>it surprises people that Stephen Leacock was an</u>

> economics professor.
>
> *If* he did not descend immediately, <u>he would die</u>.
>
> *Since* they worked a statutory holiday, <u>they were paid overtime</u>.

The comma appears in the above examples because the natural order of each sentence is reversed. When the main idea, the complete thought, appears at the start, the comma is not required:

> <u>It surprises people that Stephen Leacock was an economics professor</u> *because* he is famous for his humorous novels and short stories.
>
> <u>He would die</u> *if* he did not descend immediately.
>
> <u>They were paid overtime</u> *since* they worked a statutory holiday.

Some books add a fourth category to the classification of sentence types: the compound-complex sentence. When you combine a compound and complex sentence, you create a hybrid known as a compound-complex sentence. It has two complete thoughts and one incomplete thought.

Sentence Type Summary

1. One Complete Thought = One Simple Sentence

2. One Complete Thought + One Complete Thought = One Compound Sentence

3. One Complete Thought + One Incomplete Thought = One Complex Sentence

4. Join two complete thoughts using a comma and one of seven coordinating words: and , but , or , nor , for , yet , so.

5. Join two complete thoughts with a colon or a semicolon.

6. Join two complete thoughts with a semicolon, a transitional word from the word list, and a comma.

7. A complete thought and an incomplete thought do not require any special punctuation unless the incomplete thought comes first in the sentence.

8. Placing a subordinating word, a demoting word, in front of a complete thought makes it an incomplete thought.

9. There are specific lists of transitional words for simple, compound, and complex sentences.

10. Guide readers from idea to idea by using a variety of sentence types containing an assortment of transitional words and phrases.

8. Use Parallel Structure

When listing items, always use parallel structure.

The straightforward and effective transitional device of numbering items requires parallelism: First, second, third, or firstly, secondly, thirdly.

If the first item in the list ends with the word *it*, then the other words also end in *it*:

Prepare tofu in one of three ways: boil it, fry it, bake it.

If the first item in the list starts with *by* and the next word ends in *ing*, maintain the pattern:

Students pass courses in three ways: by attending, by reading, by studying.

Students pass courses in three ways: by attending lectures, by reading articles, by studying notes.

Compound sentences use parallel structure for integrating similar ideas or contrasting opposing ideas:

You must practice every day; you must practice every night; you must practice every moment.

I have good news, and I have bad news.

Some of them love it; some of them hate it.

Some say NIMBY, *Not in my backyard*; I say NIABY, *Not in anyone's backyard.*

Our main concern is not energy consumed; our main concern is energy wasted.

Parallelism highlights ideas and makes them memorable:

We need 4 hugs a day for survival. We need 8 hugs a day for maintenance. We need 12 hugs a day for growth (Virginia Satir).

9. Use Precise Modifiers And Verbs

When selecting modifiers and verbs, look for the perfect word, the accurate and distinctive word.

Modifiers: Adjectives And Adverbs

Employing vague adjectives and adverbs is like consuming junk food: it tastes good and is filling, but it is not nutritious.

We had a <u>good</u> sales year; we <u>really</u> beat the competition. (Vague)

We had a <u>pretty wonderful</u> vacation. (Vague)

The welding shop is <u>very</u> hot. (Vague)

Replace fuzzy modifiers such as *very, really,* or *good* with one of the following:

1. An Accurate Statistic

   Sales increased by 34.2 percent.

2. An Appropriate Comparison

   If our sales team played hockey, the Stanley Cup would

be ours.

3. A Relevant Example

On our vacation, we sailed; we snorkelled; we danced; we laughed.

4. A Creative Comparison

Working in the welding shop is like working in a sauna under a heat lamp.

5. A Distinct and Precise Modifier

The welding shop is spitefully hot.

Precise, descriptive, and inventive words or phrases always trump a vague adjective or adverb.

Vague: <u>Effective</u> information dissemination is <u>important</u>.

Precise: <u>Timely and accurate</u> information dissemination is vital.

Vague: <u>Generally</u>, the operating system works.

Precise: <u>Eight times out of ten</u>, the operating system loads correctly.

Vague: It was a <u>good</u> board meeting.

Precise: The board meeting was <u>short, productive, and congenial</u>.

Vague: It was a <u>great</u> book.

Precise: The historical novel was <u>articulate, accurate, and well-researched</u>.

Vague: <u>Most</u> of the examples are from the middle class.

Precise: <u>Eighty percent</u> of the examples are from the middle class.

Vague: This is a <u>nice</u> example of evolution at work.

Precise: This is an <u>elegant</u> example of evolution.

Vague: <u>Normally,</u> we deliver items on time.
Precise: We deliver all local packages on time <u>99% of the time</u>.

Vague: Advertisers <u>often</u> target teenagers.
Precise: Advertisers <u>relentlessly</u> target teenagers .

Vague: The eclipse was <u>pretty interesting</u>.
Precise: The eclipse was <u>awe-inspiring</u>.

Vague: We <u>really</u> need a new environmental policy.
Precise: Without a new environmental policy, <u>our company will collapse</u>.

Vague: <u>Some</u> of the managers attended the retreat.
Precise: <u>Six</u> managers attended the retreat.

Vague: <u>Sometimes</u>, yelling is appropriate.
Precise: <u>If you feel threatened</u>, yelling is appropriate.

Vague: Freud had some <u>very interesting</u> theories.
Precise: Freud's theories were <u>revolutionary</u>.

Verbs

Your verb quest parallels your modifier quest: find the appropriate, exact, and relevant word or phrase. Consider how profoundly the meaning, tone, and direction of the sentences change as the verb changes:

Psychologists <u>discuss</u> nature versus nurture.
A neutral discussion

Psychologists <u>debate</u> nature versus nurture.
A lively discussion

Psychologists <u>harp</u> on about nature versus nurture.
A boring discussion

Psychologists <u>fuss</u> over nature versus nurture.
A tedious discussion

Psychologists <u>nitpick</u> over nature versus nurture.

A tedious and boring discussion

Psychologists <u>articulate</u> the nature versus nurture debate.
A scholarly and coherent discussion

Psychologists <u>explore</u> the nature versus nurture argument.
A scientific discussion

Psychologists <u>clarify</u> the nature versus nurture argument.
A valuable discussion

Choosing specific, precise, articulate modifiers and verbs presents the reader with a clear, convincing, accurate, and distinctive message.

10. Verify Word Definitions

The reason the internet is overflowing with lists of commonly confused words is that many writers misuse common words. Take a few seconds and look up the meanings of words.

Discover if you are using the word correctly. Discover if it is even a word.

For example, many writers and speakers begin a sentence with the word *irregardless*. Look it up. It is nonstandard usage. The correct word is *regardless*.

Alright is nonstandard usage. The correct form is all right.

Perusing a book is not the same as browsing through it. When you peruse a book you examine it in detail.

Nonplussed does not mean cool and collected; it means baffled.

Enormity does not mean big; it means outrageousness.

Plethora does not mean lots; it means too much.

Disinterested does not mean uninterested; it means unbiased.

Reticent does not mean reluctant; it means disinclined to talk.

Refute does not mean debate; it means disprove.

Mettlesome does not mean interfering; it means brave.

Infer does not mean suggest; imply means suggest.

11. Simplify

Always write using plain language. This does not mean using only small words or writing in a chatty tone. It means avoiding inflated language, tortuous sentence structure, and overloaded sentences. These elements do not make you sound intelligent; they make you unintelligible.

Complex ideas call for plain language and short sentences:

> The quintessential insinuation of yawning as a symbolic mode of discourse seems to be indicative of a diminished attention span.

> Yawning signals inattention.

> This report is designed to, hopefully, incentivize the reader to contribute their own analytical critique to the ongoing discourse in this field of endeavour.

> This report welcomes and encourages readers' comments.

> Having collected and analyzed the statistically significant and relevant data over a period of some time, it seems inescapable to not conclude that our laissez faire approach to the factors aggravating climate change are further impairing the planet.

> In conclusion, I believe climate change profoundly harms the earth.

Do not make one sentence carry too much weight. Divide ideas into bite-size units of thought. If you are struggling with a sentence, divide it into two or three manageable sentences:

As technology evolves and is more readily available to the masses, it becomes an important tool that allows people alternative methods of gathering critical information outside of traditional norms, such as newspapers, radio broadcast, and television.

Accurate information distribution is a lifeline. Technology extends the reach of that lifeline beyond traditional media.

Alderman Druh Farrell: Plain Language

Druh Farrell is in her fourth term (2001 - 2013) as an Alderman in Calgary, Alberta. She was instrumental in helping the city develop and implement a Plain Language Policy. Her impressive track record of accomplishments is based in part on her highly developed communication skills.

It seems so basic, really. In order to engage in meaningful conversation, one must use language that is understood by the intended audience. Governments, in order to be effective, need to be skilled communicators. Why, then, is the use of jargon and bafflegab so commonplace in bureaucracies? And how does the liberal use of acronyms and technical terms alienate the public trust?

The use of acronyms and technical terms at the City of Calgary was making our communications unintelligible to anyone who was not an insider. Citizens would furrow their brows when we made public presentations; the terms differed from one department to another, fortifying departmental silos. At the same time we were inviting citizens to share their ideas with us.

We adopted a new Plain Language Policy to help us break the habit of using acronyms and lingo by mandating the use of clear and simple language. Why use the term fenestration, when window would do just fine, or downright nonsense like aquatic centre flat-water pool, (I'm not making that up) for swimming pool.

Simple doesn't mean simplistic. The first big test of the power of plain language came during the 2013 Flood, when boiling the message down to clear and simple terms became critical for public safety. The clarity of the message helped reassure Calgarians that matters were well in hand and bolstered the confidence that we would recover. Clear and simple became fearless and flawless.

Chapter Seven Summary - Write Concise, Confident, And Credible Sentences

Editing is about more than making your work technically correct. Vague words, unnecessary words, verb piles, and technical errors detract from your ideas and harm your credibility.

As you edit, ask yourself this: Did I avoid the use of to verbs and too many verbs? Do I know the definition of this word? Is there a more precise word than the one I am using? Is this a simple, compound, or complex sentence? Is my writing concise, confident, and correct?

EIGHT
Use A Checklist

Checklists seem lowly and simplistic, but they help fill in for the gaps in our brains and between our brains.
–Atul Gawande

Checklists help us avoid serious mistakes and omissions. But most importantly, checklists make us mindful.

Being mindful means focusing on the task at hand; it means being present in the moment. That is why pilots, astronauts, investors, lawyers, and surgeons use checklists.

The following writer's checklist taps you on the shoulder and asks, "Are you sure you know what you want to say and how you want to say it? Are you sure your readers have everything they need?"

Checklists not only ask if we tightened the bolts on the wheels; they ask if we put the wheels on the right car.

One Crucial Checklist

Knowing What To Say

☐ I found my keyword.

☐ I created a working title.

☐ I identified a one word goal.

☐ I selected a genre.

☐ I linked my goal and genre.

☐ I researched my audience.

The Introduction

☐ I have a descriptive title.

☐ I provided context.

☐ I set the stage.

☐ I stated my goal.

☐ My genre is obvious.

☐ I outlined my key idea.

☐ I listed my main points.

The Middle

☐ I used transitions.

☐ I provided evidence.

☐ My paragraphs are short.

☐ I supplied the appropriate documentation.

☐ I used graphics where appropriate.

☐ I developed my main points in the order listed in the introduction.

The Conclusion

- ☐ I created a satisfying and logical ending.
- ☐ I compared and harmonized my introduction and conclusion.

Editing

- ☐ I avoided *to* verbs.
- ☐ I avoided using too many verbs.
- ☐ I avoided contractions.
- ☐ I double checked all my possessives.
- ☐ I avoided gender specific language.
- ☐ I used periods for a full stop and commas for a pause.
- ☐ I used simple, compound, and complex sentences.
- ☐ I used parallel structure.
- ☐ My modifiers and verbs are precise.
- ☐ I checked the meanings of words.
- ☐ I simplified and used plain language.

Acknowledgements

Thank you to the following individuals for their valuable contributions.

Druh Farrell

Claudia Hammond

Judy Johnson

Sam McNerney

Clifton B. Parker

Bruce Ravelli

Emma Teitel

Jennifer Welsh

David M. Wilkinson

Thank you to the following authors and organizations for copyright permission.

Amen, Daniel
The Amen Solution: The Brain Healthy
Way to Get Thinner, Smarter, Happier
Three Rivers Press
2011
amenclinics.com

Atkinson, Nancy
Why Are Astronauts Weightless in Space?
Universe Today
May 21, 2012
universetoday.com

Basham, Elaine and Sue Sarkesian
How To Write a Bad Resume
The Resume Group
February 25, 2009
theresumegroup.blogspot.ca

Bassi, Samuela, Alex Bowen, and Sam
Fankhauser
The Case For And Against Onshore Wind
Energy In The UK
Grantham Research Institute, London
School of Economics and Political Science
June 2012
se.ac.uk

Bereziuk, Cheryl
The Gendered Brain
Lobstick
2:14, 2001
lobstick.com

Blake, William
Auguries of Innocence
The Pickering Manuscript
1803
gutenberg.org

Brotman, John
New Music for Canada
Literary Review of Canada
July/August 2012
reviewcanada.ca

Caldarella, Paul, et al.
The Effects of School-Wide Positive
Behavior Support on Middle School
Climate and Student Outcomes
RMLE Online: Research in Middle Level
Education
35:4 2011
amle.org

Cherry, Kendra
Reasons Why We Forget
About.com
n.d.
About.com

Clean Water Action
Fracking: The Process
Clean Water Action
n.d.
cleanwater.org

Curry, Timothy and Lynn Shibut
The Cost of the Savings and Loan Crisis:
Truth and Consequences
FDIC Banking Review
13:2, 2000
fdic.gov

Dauvergne, Mia, and Leonardo De Socio
Firearms and Violent Crime
Juristat
28:2, 2008
statcan.gc.ca

Davies, Stephen
On Defining Music
The Monist
95:4 October 2012
themonist.com

Development Initiatives
GHA Report 2012
Development Initiatives, Global
Humanitarian Assistance Report 2012
2012
globalhumanitarianassistance.org

Dexter, Hollye
What Is Forgiveness
Hollye Dexter
April 18, 2011
hollyedexter.blogspot.ca

DiFranco, Ani
Fire Door
Ani DiFranco
1990
righteousbabe.com

Enbridge
Benefits for British Columbians
Northern Gateway Project
n.d.
northerngateway.ca

Fenster, Ariel
Are Wind Farms Really Bad for People's
Health?
McGill Blogs
February 16, 2013
blogs.mcgill.ca

Finn, Kristin V.
Marijuana Use at School and Achievement-
Linked Behaviours
The High School Journal
95:3, 2012
uncpress.unc.edu

Fong, Francis
The Plight of Younger Workers
Observation: TD Economics
March 8, 2012
td.com

Ganz, Lowell and Babaloo Mandel
City Slickers
WB Motion Picture Rights
1991
www.warnerbros.com

Gawande, Atul
Cowboys and Pit Crews -2011 Harvard
Medical School Commencement Address
May 26, 2011
The New Yorker
May 26, 2011
newyorker.com

Gulden, Wayne
Against the Wind
Wind Farm Realities
April 28, 2010
windfarmrealities.org

Haydn, Terry
History in Schools and the Problem of
"The Nation"
MDPI Open Access Publishing
December 14, 2012
mdpi.com

Keenan, John
The Four Levels of Happiness Defined
Spitzer Center
n.d.
spitzercenter.org

Klein, Barrett A.
The Curious Connection Between Insects
and Dreams
MDPI Open Access Publishing
December 21, 2011
mdpi.com

Kolstad, Rosemarie et al.
Comparing Democratic Maturity Test
Scores For German And American College
Freshman
College Student Journal
35:1, March 2001
projectinnovation.biz

Kozhaya, Norma and Germain Belzile
Would Higher Tuition Fees Restrict Access
To University Studies?
Montreal Economic Institute
June 2010
iedm.org/e

Kozhaya, Norma
Lowering Fees Does Not Make Universities
More Accessible
Montreal Economic Institute
October 6, 2003
iedm.org/e

Leacock, Stephen
Gertrude the Governess
Nonsense Novels
1911
gutenberg.org

Lee, Marc
Enbridge Pipe Dreams and Nightmares
Canadian Centre for Policy Alternatives
March 2012
policyalternatives.ca

Lickerman, Alex
How To Remember Things
Happiness In This World
June 7, 2009
happinessinthisworld.com

Liu, Jianghong and Nicola Graves
Childhood Bullying: A Review of
Constructs, Concepts, and Nursing
Implications
Public Health Nursing
November 2011
onlinelibrary.wiley.com

MacDonald, Meredith Smith
Why I Love, Support & Believe in Wind
Energy
February 6, 2013
lifeamonggiants.com

Madore, Odette
The Canadian and American Health Care
Systems
Library of Parliament
BP-300E: June 1992
parl.gc.ca

Matlock, Erin
How To Remember Names – Five Easy
Tricks
Brain Pages Inc
n.d.
brainpagesmedia.com

Matlock, Erin
9 Reasons Golf Is Good For Your Brain
Brain Pages Inc
n.d.
brainpagesmedia.com

McNerney, Sam
Does Studying Behavioral Economics
Improve Your Financial Decisions?
Why We Reason
August 25, 2011
whywereason.com

McRaney, David
You Are Not So Smart
Gotham Books
2011
davidmcraney.com

Montaigne, Fen
Obama vs. Romney: A Stark Contrast on
the Environment
Yale Environment 360
September 17, 2012
e360.yale.edu

Nankin, Jesse and Krista Kjellman Schmidt
History of U.S. Gov't Bailouts
ProPublica
April 15, 2009
propublica.org

Nin, Anaïs
Seduction Of The Minotaur
Cities of the Interior
1959
anaisnin.com

Parker, Clifton B.
The Pursuit of Happiness
UC Davis Magazine
28:3, 2011
ucdavismagazine.ucdavis.edu

Parker, Clifton B.
The History of Happiness
UC Davis Magazine
28:3, 2011
ucdavismagazine.ucdavis.edu

Parry, Haydn
Re-Engineering Mosquitos To Fight Disease
Ted Talks
2012
ted.com

Pedder, David
Are Small Classes Better? Understanding
Relationships between Class Size,
Classroom Processes and Pupils' Learning
Oxford Review of Education
32:2, May 2006
tandfonline.com

Percic, Eva
What Kind of Blogger Are You? 7 Different
Blogger Types Explained
Zemanta
December 6, 2012
zemanta.com

Pettit, Donald A.
Introduction
The Peace: An Exploration in Photographs
2001
peacephotographics.com

Puma, Joe
Comparing Homeschooling vs Public
Schooling:
Ten Reasons for Homeschooling Children
HomeschoolingHub
homeschoolinghub.com

Ravelli, Bruce
Investigating Canadian and American
Value Differences Through an Analysis of
Media Portrayals of Native Issues
Seeing Ourselves
2010
ravelli.ca

Restak, Richard M.
The Other Difference Between Boys and
Girls
Educational Leadership
1979
ascd.org

Rich, Simona
What Is Guilt?
Personal Development Coach
n.d.
personal-development-coach.net

Rosado, Caleb
Toward a Definition of Multiculturalism
Rosado Consulting for Change in Human
Systems
1997
rosado.net

Rosenbloom, Eric
A Problem with Wind Power
AWEO
September 5, 2006
aweo.org

Satir, Virginia
Virginia Satir Global Network
n.d.
satirglobal.org/

Scarf, Maggie
The Happiness Syndrome
The New Republic
December 5, 1994
newrepublic.com

Schnee, Chadwick
Stewart Provides Much Needed Laughter
Campus Times
December 9, 2001
campustimes.org

Scott, Jared
Tablet Vs Ereader—Which Is Better For You
Outside's Go
March 17, 2011
outsidego.com

Scott, Julia
A Cost Comparison of Home Brew Vs.
Store-Bought Beer
July 10, 2012
mint.com/blog

Scott, Matthew
What is Charisma? How To Be Charismatic
Skills You Need
n.d.
skillsyouneed.com

Shepherd, Michael and Carolyn Watters
The Evolution of Cybergenres
HICSS '98 Proceedings of the Thirty-First
Annual Hawaii International Conference on
System Sciences - Volume 2
1998
ieee-pes.org

Sierra, Stuart
The Three Types of Computer User
Digital Digressions
July 12, 2006
stuartsierra.com

Slootweg, J.G. and W.L. Kling
Is The Answer Blowing In The Wind?
Power and Energy Magazine
Nov.-Dec. 2003
1:6
ieee-pes.org

Strunk William, Jr.
Omit Needless Words
The Elements Of Style
1920
gutenberg.org

Sobel, Dava
Introduction
Longitude: The True Story of a Lone
Genius Who Solved the Greatest Scientific
Problem of His Time
1995
davasobel.com

Suzuki, David
A Planet for the Taking
Canadian Forum
February 1985
davidsuzuki.org

Suzuki, David
The Beauty Of Wind Farms
New Scientist
April 16, 2005
newscientist.com

Swanton, Dale N., Cynthia M. Gooch,
and Matthew S. Matell
Averaging of Temporal Memories by Rats
Journal of Experimental Psychology:
Animal Behavior Processes
35:3 July 2009
psycnet.apa.org

UBC
Student Conduct and Discipline
UBC Vancouver Academic Calendar
2013/14
calendar.ubc.ca

Ueland, Brenda
If You Want to Write: A Book about Art,
Independence and Spirit
BN Publishing
2008 (1938)
bnpublishing.com

Welsh, Jennifer
Dinosaur Farts May Have Warmed Ancient
Earth
Live Science
May 7, 2012
Livescience.com

Wilkinson, David M., Euan G. Nisbet, and
Graeme D. Ruxton
Could Methane Produced By Sauropod
Dinosaurs Have Helped Drive Mesozoic
Climate Warmth?
Current Biology
22:9, May 8, 2012
cell.com

Wise, Jeff
Your Rebel Brain
Outside's Go
n.d.
outsidego.com

Yarrow, Alder
Food and Wine Pairing is Just a Big Scam
March 12, 2008
vinography.com

For Avery, Kate, Jason and Terri

CPSIA information can be obtained at www.ICGtesting.com
Printed in the USA
LVOW05s1229070414

380649LV00052B/1053/P